HPBooks

How to Photograph

Water Sports & Activities

Rick & Susan Sammon

Publisher: Rick Bailey
Editorial Director: Theodore DiSante
Editor: Vernon Gorter
Art Director: Don Burton
Book Design: Kathleen Koopman
Typography: Cindy Coatsworth, Michelle Claridge
Photography: Rick and Susan Sammon, unless otherwise credited

Published by HPBooks®, P.O. Box 5367, Tucson, AZ 85703. (602) 888-2150
ISBN: 0-89586-273-5 Library of Congress Catalog No. 84-80395

Photo by Harry Benson.

Contents

Introduction

This book is a result of our love for the water. We have both enjoyed many vacations, weekends and days off in, around and under water.

We enjoy swimming, no matter whether it's in a pool, lake, stream or ocean. Fishing, rowing, sailing, water skiing and canoeing all fascinate us. Trained creatures at water shows and wild animals in the great outdoors make us reach for our cameras. Whenever possible, we like to catch a sunrise or sunset at the ocean.

There's a special excitement about the underwater environment. Diving gives the sensation of weightlessness—like floating in outer space, with few restrictions on your movements. The beautiful, colorful fish and corals that comprise a coral reef are breathtaking to observe.

Generally, water scenes offer both relaxation and excitement. They offer unlimited picture-taking opportunities and challenges, too.

The material for this book grew almost imperceptibly. Since our marriage, nearly a decade ago, we've spent much time traveling the world. We're always drawn naturally to the water—and our file of photos keeps growing.

In 1980, we started scuba diving and became involved with *CEDAM International,* a club dedicated to Conservation, Education, Diving, Archeology and Museums. We've spent several vacations perfecting our underwater photography techniques. At the time of writing, Rick is president of *CEDAM International.* Susan is publisher of the *CEDAM International Bulletin.*

Because the water environment presents unique photographic challenges, we find it especially satisfying when our pictures are successful.

We've learned a great deal from personal experimentation. We have also been fortunate to have good friends such as Robert Farber, Harry Benson, Lucien Clergue, Lou Jones, John Isaac and Patricia Caulfield. All these professional photographers have shared some of their "secrets" with us. They've also provided some of their images for use in this book.

On the technical side, our editor, Vernon Gorter, has been a super help. Although he now lives in the desert, where water scenes are rare, his understanding of photography and its technology has helped us communicate our ideas to you effectively.

We hope that our experiences will help you to get the kind of pictures you want. If you read the text carefully and apply what you learn, you should be able to capture those special moments on film.

We realize the value of a clean and unspoiled water environment. We know that much of the damage done to it is irreversible. Therefore, we are actively concerned with preserving clean oceans, lakes, rivers and streams. Please do the same.

And, lots of happy and safe shooting!

Rick and Susan Sammon

COVER PHOTOS
Front: Sailboat—Lou Jones
Woman—Robert Farber
Scuba Diver—Rick Sammon
Back: Lucien Clergue

1 Equipment

If you start out with the right equipment, you'll have the best chance of getting the great photographs you're after. If you buy right the first time, you'll also save money in the long run.

In this chapter, the *Basic Camera System* section gives you a good overview of cameras, lenses and accessories for use in and around water. *Waterproof and Weatherproof Equipment* describes what you'll need to make pictures under water or in very wet conditions. *Care and Maintenance* shows you how to protect your equipment and possibly avoid costly repairs.

At the end of the book, you'll find a list of major manufacturers and distributors of weatherproof and waterproof cameras and accessories. If you want more information on a product we discuss, contact the manufacturer or distributor or see your local photo dealer. We have dealt with most of the companies we've listed and have found them very helpful in answering our questions.

The combined assets of versatility and portability make a 35mm SLR system ideal for the kind of photography discussed in this book. You are not likely to need everything shown in this picture. Before you buy equipment, determine your specific needs and what your budget can bear.

BASIC CAMERA SYSTEM

Putting together a 35mm camera system requires thought and planning. Before you purchase a camera, ask yourself these questions: Does the camera body offer all the features I want? Can I add a lens system that will meet my shooting requirements? Are accessories readily available? Can I *afford* all the lenses and accessories I'll need?

HPBooks has published comprehensive manuals on the Canon, Minolta, Nikon, Olympus and Pentax camera systems. We recommend you take a careful look at these books. A reputable camera dealer can also help you decide which system is best for you. In addition, you can find useful information on 35mm SLR cameras in various monthly photography magazines.

CAMERA BODY

The camera body is the basic component of a 35mm SLR camera system. Here are some of the features you should evaluate:

Handling—A camera should feel comfortable and natural in your hands. Some models feature contoured fingergrips that make holding the camera easier. Vinyl or rubber coverings can give you a firmer grip on a camera.

It's possible to take excellent photographs around water with modest equipment. When you look at this picture, you can't tell whether it was made with an expensive SLR or a simple fixed-lens camera. But you can tell it was taken by an observant, capable photographer. Photo by Harry Benson.

Weight—We like lightweight equipment because we're always changing position, looking for a better angle or viewpoint. Compactness and portability are especially important because we like to have several camera bodies and lenses with us. Usually, if the camera body is light, the lenses will be, too.

Exposure Control—Today's popular 35mm SLRs feature sophisticated electronic metering systems that help you get great pictures. However, each exposure-control method has its advantages and disadvantages. Read this section carefully, to see which method meets your preferences and shooting requirements.

• *Manual-exposure control* means that you select and set both shutter speed and aperture for correct exposure. This may take several seconds, which could mean the difference between a great picture and no picture at all. However, with manual-exposure control you do have *total* creative control of aperture and shutter speed.

• *Aperture-priority* means that you select the aperture and the camera automatically provides the corresponding shutter speed for correct exposure. In this mode you can control depth of field quickly and easily with the aperture ring.

• *Shutter-priority* provides for you to select the shutter speed. The camera automatically selects the corresponding aperture for correct exposure. If you want to either "freeze" or blur a subject by selecting a fast or slow shutter speed, shutter-priority automation is a useful feature. This mode is great for shooting fast-paced sporting events.

• *Programmed control* means that the camera automatically selects aperture and shutter speed. All you do is point, focus and shoot. When you want the camera to "do all the thinking" for you, shoot in the programmed mode. With programmed control, you won't know what the shutter-speed or aperture settings are unless the viewfinder has a full display of this information. Therefore, you may have no control over depth of field or stopping subject movement.

• *Multimode cameras* feature two or three of the above methods of exposure control. These cameras offer the advantage of switching modes for different shooting situations.

No exposure mode is perfect for every shooting situation. In fact, two photographers may choose two different exposure modes for the same shooting situation.

There are about 50 different lenses here, all from one camera manufacturer. Other manufacturers offer similar lines. You can have all the versatility you're likely to need by carefully choosing three or four from this selection.

In this scene, most of the light is coming from the sun, which is near the edge of the picture area. A center-weighted averaging meter will only register a fraction of this light. This could lead to overexposure and a transparency with a washed-out look. With a scene like this, bracket exposures liberally.

Why? Because exposure-control methods are largely a matter of personal preference.

You should think about the kinds of photos you'll be taking and make your own decision on that basis.

Viewfinder—Most current SLRs have full-information viewfinders. All the information important to taking a picture is displayed. This includes aperture setting, shutter speed and exposure mode—aperture priority, shutter priority, manual or programmed. A camera may have a liquid-crystal display (LCD), light-emitting diode (LED) display or match needle. If you want to know what your camera has "on its mind," make sure it has a full-information viewfinder.

LENS SYSTEM

Major 35mm SLR manufacturers offer a wide selection of lenses for their cameras. Independent lens manufacturers offer more. The available lenses range in focal length from 7.5mm to 1600mm. Here's a look at some of the more useful lenses:

Standard Lens—Lenses in the 45-58mm range are usually referred to as *standard.* In normal use, these lenses reproduce the perspective of a scene much as you see it from the camera position. A standard lens is a good first lens and a good general-purpose lens. You can use it for shooting landscapes and seascapes, for pictures of animals that are close to you, for glamour photography and for general people photography.

As all lenses, the standard lens has its limitations. However, we've found that, of the 18 lenses we have, the 50mm is the *right* one much of the time.

Wide-Angle Lens—The wider the angle of view of a lens, the more of the scene you can capture from the same viewpoint. Wide-angle lenses are divided into three categories: 28-35mm medium-wide-angle, 21-24mm super-wide-angle and 17-20mm ultra-wide-angle.

As the focal length decreases, depth of field at each *f*-stop increases. For example, with a 24mm lens you'll get more depth of field at *f*-8 than you would with a 35mm lens at *f*-8 from the same distance. If you want to capture a wide scene in sharp focus, use an ultra-wide-angle lens and shoot at a small *f*-stop.

Wide-angle lenses also increase the apparent distance between foreground and background. A relatively small pond can look quite large when photographed up close with a super-wide-angle lens.

Wide-angle lenses are ideal for photographing people in their environment when your own movement is limited. For example, if you're on a sailboat and want to photograph boat, captain and

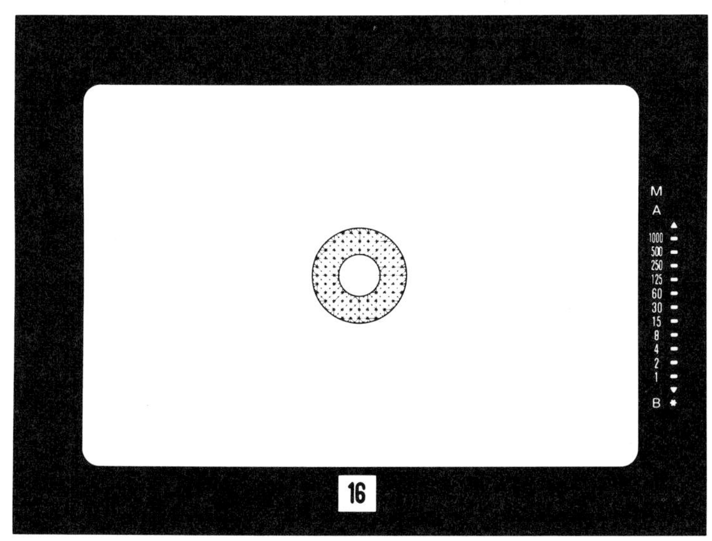

This is a typical full-information viewfinder. All the data you need to control picture-taking is shown: Manual (M) and Automatic (A) exposure indicators, shutter-speed setting, lens aperture and over- and underexposure warning signals.

Sunset silhouettes can make very effective pictures. Usually, you'll get a surprisingly good result by simply giving the meter-indicated exposure. However, to get the color and tone of the sky just right, bracket exposures freely—up to two steps in either direction.

crew, a lens in the 17-24mm range will prove very useful. If you are photographing a model on the beach or by a pool, you'll probably want to include some background and foreground. Use a wide-angle lens. However, avoid wide-angle lenses for full-frame portraits. At close range, facial features become distorted and appear unflattering.

As you'll learn later in the book, objects under water appear closer than they actually are. This means they also appear larger. To include the entire subject in the picture, you need a correspondingly wider angle of view. For this reason, wide-angle lenses are very popular among underwater photographers.

Telephoto Lens—Telephoto lenses can be divided into four categories: 75-85mm short telephoto, 100-200mm medium telephoto, 300-600mm long telephoto and 1000-1600mm super telephoto.

Telephoto lenses are useful *distance eliminators.* They bring you closer to your subject when you actually can't—or don't want to—approach the subject. For example, you may want to photograph a child without attracting his attention. You'll get an unimpressively small image with a 50mm lens from 20 feet away. If you stay in the same position and shoot with a 135mm lens, you'll get a frame-filling image of the child. With a 300mm lens, you can get a detailed head shot.

You'll need a telephoto lens for photographing animals, mammals and fish in water shows, sports action and wildlife. A short- or medium-telephoto lens is also useful for making professional-looking glamour photographs and portraits. It enables you to get sufficiently far from the subject to avoid unflattering distortion.

Depth of field at each *f*-stop decreases as lens focal length increases. For example, if you're photographing a subject 25 feet away with a 400mm lens set at *f*-8, you have less depth of field than if you were photographing from the same distance with a 100mm lens at *f*-8.

Zoom Lens—A zoom lens is a variable-focal-length lens. It provides you with a selection of focal lengths without the need to carry several lenses. There are 24-35mm wide-angle zooms, 35-105mm wide-angle to medium-telephoto zooms, 75-200mm short- to medium-telephoto zooms and 200-500mm medium- to long-telephoto zooms.

Zoom lenses are generally heavier than fixed-focal-length lenses. Except with the best and most expensive zoom lenses, you may sometimes notice a slight falloff in sharpness and brightness toward image corners.

We use two zoom lenses regularly—a 35-105mm and a 75-200mm. We find these lenses particularly helpful for photographing water shows, wildlife and sports action.

Fisheye Lens—This is an ultra-wide-angle lens. There are two basic types of fisheye lenses. The

For shooting general scenic views like this while you're traveling, the standard 50mm lens is ideal. It gives a sufficiently wide field of view and enough depth of field to ensure that you take home a record of that unrepeatable experience. When you have a chance to stop and compose the scene as you want it, having a selection of other focal lengths helps.

16mm full-frame fisheye produces an image that fills the entire rectangular 35mm frame. The 7.5mm and 8mm fisheye lenses give a circular image in the center of the 35mm film frame.

Fisheye lenses offer tremendous depth of field. For example, if you set the 16mm lens to an aperture of *f*-22, you'll get everything in focus from infinity to just a few inches in front of the lens.

Straight lines that do not pass through the center of the image area will reproduce curved. Thus, if you tilt the camera downward and photograph the horizon, the horizon line will appear curved—and the earth will look truly round! When you place the horizon in the center of the frame, it'll appear straight again. The farther you place the line from the center of the frame, the more curved it will become.

The circular-image fisheye lens offers a 180° angle of view. If you lie on your back at the beach and point the camera straight up, you can record the entire visible sky on one film frame.

Mirror Lens—Also known as a *catadioptric* lens, a mirror lens uses a combination of lenses and mirrors to form an image. A mirror lens is lighter and physically shorter than a conventional telephoto lens of the same focal length. This compactness makes a mirror lens easy to carry and hold.

Mirror lenses are available in focal lengths of 250mm, 500mm, 600mm, 800mm and 1000mm. Each lens has a fixed aperture. You have to control exposure by varying the shutter speed or by using neutral-density filters. You have no depth-of-field control.

Macro Lens—Macro lenses let you get large images of small subjects because they allow very close focusing. Some lenses can even give a life-size image.

Macro lenses for 35mm SLRs are available in focal lengths of 50mm and 100mm. Nikon makes 55mm and 105mm macro lenses. The 100mm and 105mm lenses have a slightly longer minimum working distance. Macro lenses can be used for general photography, too. A 50mm is a good standard lens; a 100mm serves as a medium-telephoto lens.

A macro lens enables you to get large images of small objects without additional camera accessories. This lens is also suitable for general photography—a great advantage if you like to travel light.

Here are some accessories that enable you to use an SLR to its full potential. 1) With a motor drive, you can shoot action photos in rapid succession. 2) Electronic flash can often improve outdoor photographs by brightening shadows and reducing image contrast. 3) A power charger shortens the recycling time between flashes. 4) This infrared remote-control set permits you to operate the camera shutter from a distance. 5) A multi-function back can be programmed to take sequence pictures at predetermined time intervals up to hours and even days. It also imprints time and date directly on the film.

ACCESSORIES

Throughout this book we discuss accessories that we use. Here is a brief look at some of the important ones:

Motor Drive and Auto Winder—Motor drives and auto winders automatically advance the film after each exposure. Motor drives, however, also operate the shutter at a pre-selected repeat rate. In addition, motor drives advance the film at a faster continuous rate and feature power rewind.

Electronic Flash—Flash units are helpful for shooting at indoor water shows, swimming pools and aquariums. Flash is also useful for adding fill light to shadows when shooting outdoors. Electronic flash is also invaluable in underwater photography, as we'll show later.

There are manual and automatic flash units. Some automatic units can be set for manual operation, too.

Manual flash units require that you set the aperture for correct exposure at each shooting distance. With automatic units, you set the aperture just once. Light output is controlled automatically to give correct exposure within a specific distance range. We prefer automatic flash control because we can then direct our thinking exclusively to the picture-taking.

You'll find additional information about underwater flash later in this chapter.

Tripod—When we are shooting with a telephoto lens, we use a heavy-duty tripod to hold the camera secure and steady. For macro work, we use a lightweight mini-tripod. This compact unit is about six inches long when folded and easily fits in our camera bag.

Filters—Listed below are some filter types that are useful for photography in the water environment. These and other filters are discussed more fully in the *Shooting at the Beach* chapter.

- A *polarizing filter* enables you to darken parts of a blue sky and thereby emphasize white clouds. With this filter, you can also reduce glare on sand, remove reflections from water and increase color saturation in a scene. You can use this filter with b&w and color film.
- With a *skylight filter* you can reduce a blue color cast caused by ultraviolet (UV) radiation and blue skylight. This filter can never harm your photos. For this

reason, it makes a good permanent lens protector. You can leave it on the camera at all times. It's safer and easier to clean than the front lens surface. And, in case of damage, it is certainly less costly to replace than a front lens element.

- *Creative filters* can change day into night, gray sky into blue sky, produce starbursts and rainbows, and much more. There are enough creative filters available to enable you to change a scene in many different ways. Ask your photo dealer to show you what's available.
- *Color-compensating (CC) filters* enable you to control individual color imbalances. They are available in cyan, magenta, yellow, red, green and blue, and in densities ranging from 0.05 to 0.50. CC filters are identified by type, density and color, in that order. For example, a CC filter that has a density of 0.20 and is yellow is called a *CC20Y* filter.
- To slightly change the color temperature of the light, use *light-balancing filters.* Filters in the 82 series are bluish. They increase the color temperature of the light, making the illumination more bluish. Filters in the 81 series are amber. They make the illumination more reddish.
- *Color-conversion filters* are similar to light-balancing filters, but stronger. They correct for a spectral imbalance in the illumination. With them, you can convert tungsten lighting for use with a daylight-balanced color film. Alternatively, you can convert daylight for use with a tungsten-balanced film. Filters in the 80 series are blue and increase the color temperature of a light source. Filters in the 85 series are amber and decrease the color temperature of light.

Camera Bag—There are many different camera bags from which you can choose. They come in all colors, sizes and shapes. Some have adjustable and removable inside pockets or compartments. Some are well padded.

Before you buy a camera bag, consider what equipment you'll need to carry and make sure it will all fit. If you are like most avid photographers, you'll end up with more than one bag. We have three.

One accommodates a single camera body and two lenses. Another accepts two bodies and five lenses. The largest bag holds two camera bodies, eight lenses, several filters and a mini-tripod. Each of the bags has additional room for plenty of film.

WATERPROOF AND WEATHERPROOF EQUIPMENT

Because of the increasing popularity of scuba diving and underwater photography, there is a wide variety of underwater cameras, lenses and accessories from which you can choose. The equipment ranges from the super-sophisticated to the extremely simple. There are cameras and camera systems to fit your specific needs and budget.

FUN CAMERAS

Before we discuss the more advanced 35mm equipment, you should know that there are several waterproof and weatherproof plastic-housed 110-format and 35mm cameras. These cameras don't accept many accessories, don't offer sophisticated exposure-control systems and don't feature interchangeable lenses. However, you can have a lot of fun with them and take good pictures.

Sea & Sea Pocket Marine—This 110-format camera won't leak, even at a depth of 150 feet. It will float to the surface if you accidentally let go of it while diving. The camera features manual and automatic exposure, has a built-in

Several "fun" cameras are available for shooting snapshots in and around water. However, the capabilities of such cameras are limited. Most feature a fixed lens and accept few or no accessories.

If you own an SLR, you can easily adapt it for underwater use by sealing it in an EWA Marine Housing. The flexible plastic housing shown will not leak, even at a depth of 150 feet. At this depth, compression of the housing does not hinder easy operation of the camera.

auto winder and accepts an accessory electronic flash unit. The fixed-focus 20mm *f*-4 lens gives a sharp image at a minimum distance of 40 inches under water. By adding the Sea & Sea macro kit, you can shoot macro photos as close as five inches away.

Minolta Weathermatic-A—When you're snorkeling at relatively shallow depths—no deeper than 15 feet—this 110-format camera will give you good results. At a depth greater than 15 feet the camera may leak.

The camera features a built-in flash, a five-zone focus-control knob and a three-position exposure control—*sunny, cloudy* and *flash.* The camera floats to the surface when released under water.

Hanimex 35mm Amphibian and Sea & Sea Motor Marine—These two 35mm cameras have the same specifications: 35mm *f*-2.8 lens, maximum depth of 150 feet, manual focus, motorized film advance and built-in flash. In addition, both cameras accept an accessory close-up lens and flash.

The cameras don't offer the versatility of interchangeable lenses and the built-in flash isn't very powerful. This limits your picture-taking possibilities.

Ricoh AD-1 and Cosina Marina—These are standard 35mm cameras in watertight housings. In this respect they differ from the cameras just listed, which are specifically designed for underwater photography. Both the Ricoh and the Cosina feature a 35mm lens, automatic film advance and automatic exposure control. You can dive to 100 feet with these cameras.

The accessory electronic flash is more powerful, recycles more rapidly and gives more flashes per battery set than the other units mentioned. However, you're still limited to one lens.

Kodak 4000 Disc Camera—Cheri Sea Systems, Inc. makes a clear plastic underwater housing especially for this camera.

Fuji HD-S—This camera *can't* be used *under* water. However, its rubber-sealed construction makes it a watertight camera for shooting in an immediate water environment. Splashes won't damage it. It's a rugged camera with a rubber and plastic casing and can take a beating if knocked around on a boat or in the surf.

The Nikonos, right, is an underwater camera. It requires no additional housing. At left is a regular SLR. It requires an underwater housing, center. Each type of equipment has advantages and disadvantages, as described in the text.

HOUSING OR NIKONOS?

For the highest-quality underwater photographs and maximum versatility, you have two choices. You can shoot with a camera in an underwater housing or you can use the Nikonos IV-A system, designed for use under water without a housing. Each has its advantages and disadvantages.

The Nikonos system is lightweight and compact, while separate housings are big and bulky. However, with a housing you view the scene through the lens of your SLR, which ensures accurate framing. With the Nikonos, you view the scene through a *framefinder,* so framing isn't always totally accurate.

Cost is another consideration. If you already own a 35mm SLR and several lenses, it's cheaper for you to buy a housing for your equipment. If you don't already own suitable equipment, the Nikonos may be a better choice.

We prefer a housing over the Nikonos because we have a full lens system for our 35mm SLR cameras. When we go on a diving trip, we use the one system for our over- and underwater pictures.

When you've read the following descriptions of underwater housings and the Nikonos system, you should have a good idea of what's best for your shooting purposes.

NIKONOS SYSTEM

In 1951, Jacques Cousteau, co-inventor of the *aqualung,* had a dream he shared with Belgian aeronautical engineer Jean de Wouters. The dream was to develop a camera that could be used under water without a housing. Eight years later, a camera named the *Calypsophoto* was produced in France.

With the proper equipment, it's as easy to take portraits under water as on dry land.

The camera was an immediate hit with sports divers around the world. In 1963, Nikon purchased the manufacturing and distribution rights to the camera. It was renamed the *Nikonos.*

The camera has gone through several design changes since its introduction. The original manual-exposure camera has been updated to feature automatic exposure control. In addition, accessories such as an automatic electronic flash and wide-angle and close-up lenses have helped to make this the most popular underwater camera available.

Camera Body—The Nikonos IV-A and Nikonos V look and feel similar to standard 35mm cameras. In fact, the shutter and winder mechanism are those of the Nikon EM 35mm SLR. The Nikonos cameras feature conveniently placed exposure controls, shutter-release button, film-advance lever, film-speed dial and a bright viewfinder. The cameras are sealed at 16 locations with "O" rings. These rubber gaskets, when greased with silicone, form a tight seal against water.

Shutter speeds in the Nikonos range from eight seconds to 1/1000 second in the automatic mode. There is also a manual setting of 1/90 second plus a B setting for time exposures. The 1/90-second shutter speed doesn't require battery power. So, if you're diving at 100 feet and your battery goes dead, you can switch to the 1/90-second setting and go on shooting.

Flash-sync speed on the IV-A is 1/90 second. If you are using the Nikonos SB 101 electronic flash, discussed later in this section, the camera will automatically set the sync speed. With any other flash, simply set the exposure control dial to M. This will set the shutter to 1/90 second.

The Nikonos V is the first underwater camera to feature automatic through-the-lens (TTL) flash control. It achieves this with the Nokonos SB-102 Speedlight.

Viewfinder—Viewing the subject through the camera's viewfinder is relatively easy on land. However, when you're wearing a diving mask it becomes difficult to view a subject through the small eyepiece. You'll need either an open framefinder or a special optical viewfinder.

Framefinders, usually made of rubber or plastic, are relatively inexpensive. However, framing isn't totally accurate because you're not viewing the subject through the lens. If the finder bends out of shape, the framing will be even less accurate.

Special optical viewfinders are more accurate but also more expensive. They usually feature *parallax-correction* marks. These help to make framing much more accurate when you're shooting less than three feet from the subject.

The drawback to most separate finders is that they can be used with only one lens. For example, a 15mm optical viewfinder matches only a 15mm lens. However, some finders have accessory inserts that you can change as you change lenses.

Lenses—Four Nikonos lenses are made specifically for the Nikonos cameras. All lenses feature easy-to-reach focusing and *f*-stop knobs.

The lenses—15mm, 28mm, 35mm and 80mm—should meet all your shooting requirements. The 15mm lens is ideal for por-

Underwater photography was not common at the turn of the century. In fact, the only person remembered for his activities in this field at that time is Louis Boutan, sometimes called *the father of underwater photography.* The camera shown, made in 1900, was used by Boutan.

traits of divers, medium-size fish, views of coral gardens and even close-ups.

A 15mm focal length may seem short to you for these purposes. However, you must remember that objects under water appear considerably closer—and therefore larger—than they actually are. For this reason, the additional angular coverage is generally welcome. In order to get the clearest possible image under water, it is advisable to get as close to the subject as possible. This is another good reason for the wide-angle lens.

The 15mm lens is the most popular among professional and advanced amateur underwater photographers. It's our favorite, too. But you can't use this lens on land. It has a *dome port*, designed specifically for underwater use. The dome port is described a little later in this chapter.

Two versions of the 15mm lens are currently available. They have the same basic specifications. However, with the older model you can't use the camera's automatic exposure-metering system. That's because the rear lens barrel intrudes into the light-metering path in the camera. If you want to make use of the camera's meter, be sure to get the newer version of this lens. Discuss your need with your photo dealer.

Next in popularity among underwater photographers is the 28mm lens. It also has a slightly curved port and, therefore, won't give good results on land. Under water, it's great for photos of fish and divers.

The effect of the 35mm lens under water is about the same as that of the 50mm lens on land. That's because, as mentioned before, things appear closer under water than on land. This lens offers less depth of field than the two lenses already discussed. You must, therefore, focus accurately to get a sharp picture. In contrast to the other two lenses, this one has a *flat port*. The function of the flat port is described a little later in this chapter.

For reasons that are now clear, the 80mm lens functions underwater about as a 100mm lens would on land. It's used only rarely by underwater photographers because of the shallow depth of field it gives. For example, at six feet and *f*-11 depth of field is only about 16 inches. This lens also has a flat port.

You may be wondering about changing lenses under water. The answer is simple. You can't do it!

Nikonos Close-Up Kit—The kit contains a close-up lens that fits directly over the 28mm, 35mm or 80mm Nikonos lens. There's also a wireframe viewfinder for each of these lenses. You simply frame the subject in the appropriate viewfinder and shoot.

The simplicity of this accessory

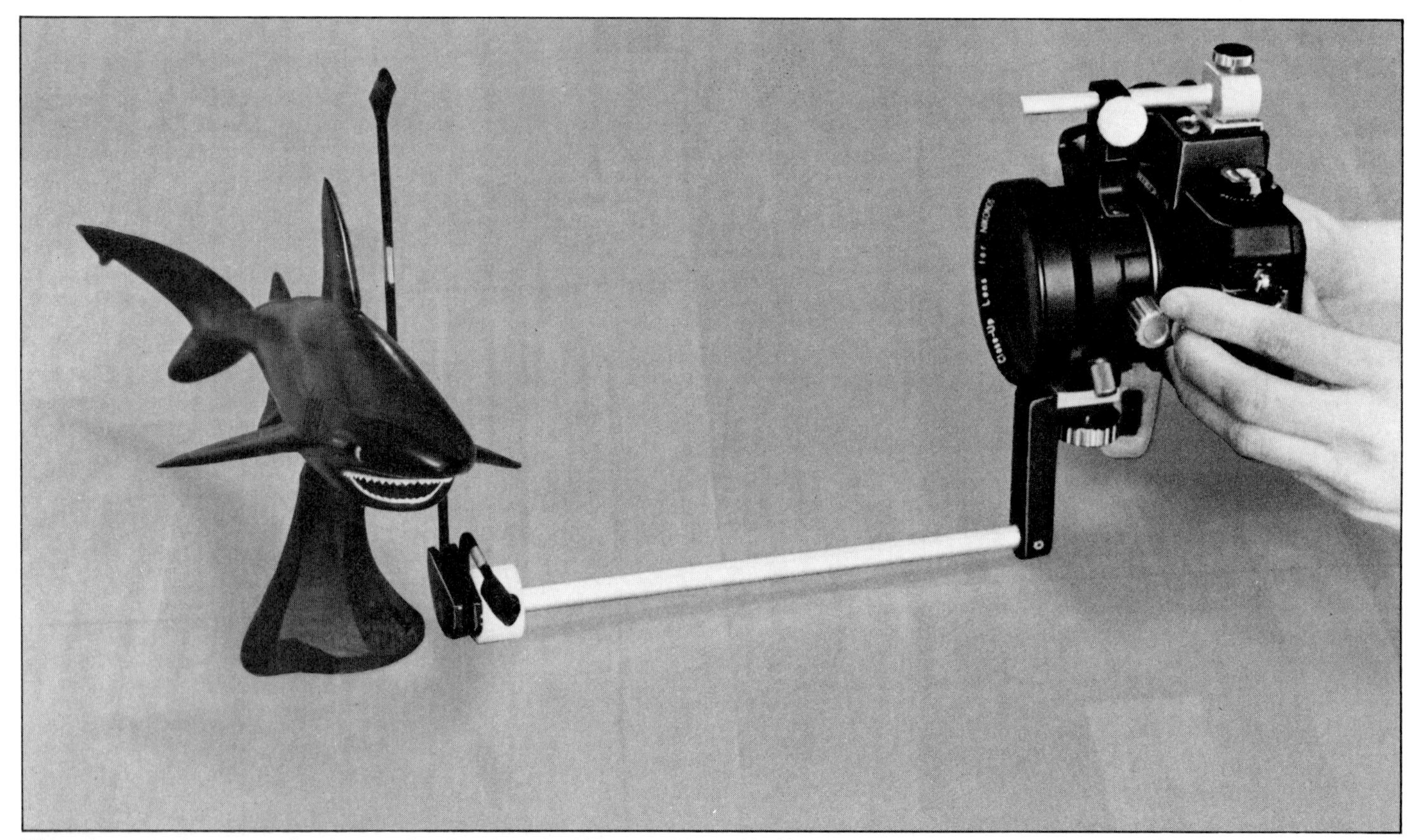

This above-water example shows clearly what the Nikonos Close-Up Kit is designed to do under water. For accurate control of subject distance, there's a wire frame for each Nikonos lens. It permits you to frame a subject quickly and accurately. When sold, the frames are full rectangles. We removed the top and one side of our frames. This enables us to position a flash to one side or above the subject without having to worry about unwanted shadows of the frame on the subject. This is a good example of how you can sometimes adapt equipment to suit your specific preferences.

makes it attractive to underwater photographers. The kit can be assembled and dismantled under water. This enables you to shoot close-ups and more distant scenes of divers and fish on the same dive.

With the close-up kit, you must use electronic flash and shoot at the smallest aperture of *f*-22 to ensure adequate depth of field. Total depth of field at *f*-22 is as follows: Three inches with the 28mm lens, 1-3/4 inches with the 35mm lens and 1/2 inch with the 80mm lens. For most of our close-up photographs we use the 28mm or 35mm lens. With the 80mm lens the depth of field is just too shallow.

Nikonos SB-101 Electronic Flash—This flash unit can be used on manual, at full power, or on either of two automatic modes. In addition, a 1/4-power setting is useful for fill light or when only a small amount of light is needed.

The flash sensor can be mounted in the shoe of the Nikonos camera. If you already have a framefinder in the shoe, you can mount the sensor next to the camera by means of a bracket that is also included with the flash.

At the full-power setting, you'll get about 100 flashes from a set of eight AA alkaline batteries. At the 1/4-power setting, you'll get about 300 flashes.

The flash unit has a quick-release bracket for easy off-camera use. Also included with the flash is an accessory diffuser. With the diffuser, the flash covers the angle of view of the 28mm lens. Without the diffuser, the flash coverage matches the angle of view of the 35mm lens.

Other Nikonos Accessories—There are many useful accessories for the Nikonos. Here's a look at just a few that can expand the versatility of this camera:

- *Aquacraft Novatek 20 Adapter* is an accessory lens. It fits over the Nikonos 35mm lens and converts it to a 20mm wide-angle lens. The adapter can be attached and removed under water, so you can shoot wide-angle and medium-wide-angle shots on the same dive.
- *Extension tubes* enable you to capture the beauty of the reef close-up, just as the close-up kit does. Aquacraft and Nikon manufacture extension tubes that will give you image magnifications from 0.3 to 2.0 (twice life size). Framefinders come with the extension tubes. They help you frame the subject quickly, easily and accurately.

Extension tubes fit between camera body and lens. You can't add or remove them under water.

- *Sea & Sea Widelenses,* available in 20mm and 18mm focal lengths, attach to the Nikonos body in the same way as the Nikonos lenses. Both lenses permit full use of the camera's metering system. They offer more extensive depth of field than the Nikonos 28mm and 35mm lenses. If you want to shoot with a wide-angle lens but can't afford the Nikonos 15mm, either of these lenses is a good alternative.
- *Flash units* for underwater photography are available, complete with mounting arms and tray. Most currently available underwater flash units can be fitted to the Nikonos camera. Sonic Research makes a relatively compact flash/arm/tray assembly designed for macro work. A metal tray holds the camera and two small electronic flash.

For illuminating large subjects under water, you can buy high-power automatic or manual flash.

UNDERWATER HOUSINGS

If you own a Canon, Nikon, Minolta, Pentax, Olympus or almost any other popular 35mm SLR, there's a housing made for it.

In a housing with a suitable port, you can use fisheye, wide-angle, macro and standard lenses. For more details, see *Dome Ports* and *Flat Ports,* page 16. Longer lenses may also fit, but they are generally cumbersome to use under water.

In choosing a housing, there are several factors to consider:

Metal or Plastic—There are three basic differences between metal and plastic housings: 1) Metal housings are three to four times more expensive than the plastic

This photo shows approximately how much you'll get in the 35mm frame with various camera lenses. The camera was about 9 feet from the diver.

To record all colors at a depth of more than a few feet, flash is essential. By daylight, this yellow and blue angel fish would have photographed blue, with no other colors present.

type. 2) Plastic housings are more buoyant and need to be weighted to prevent them from rising to the surface of the water. 3) With a clear plastic housing, you can detect a leak immediately. With a metal housing, the only way to check for a leak is by looking through the clear port or the eyepiece.

Plastic housings are more popular, mainly because of their lower cost. We prefer the metal version because we do a lot of diving and our cameras get heavy usage. We've been down to 115 feet with our housed cameras. Our housings have even endured baggage handling at airports—and survived!

Focusing—You can have focusing difficulties with a housing because your face mask prevents you from getting closer than about three inches from the eyepiece. For easier and more accurate focusing and composition, make sure your housing accepts an oversized viewfinder or eyepiece magnifier. These accessories will make all the difference in the world when you are trying to focus. In some cases, you may need a different back for the housing to accommodate this kind of accessory.

Automatic Film Advance—Another factor to consider is whether the housing accepts a motor drive or auto winder. These accessories help you capture action sequences under water. We always shoot with a motor drive. This lets us concentrate on the action we see in the viewfinder. We need not worry about finding the film-advance lever, advancing the film one frame and framing the subject again.

Dome Ports and Flat Ports—The port is the window in the housing through which the camera "sees." Two types of ports are available for underwater housings. They are *dome ports* and *flat ports.* They differ in the following important ways:

A *flat port* does not compensate for the refraction that makes objects under water appear closer and larger than they actually are. This means that a 50mm lens behind a flat port behaves as if its effective focal length were about 70mm under water. A 35mm lens has the approximate effective focal length of a 50mm lens under water. Similarly, a 28mm lens has about the effective focal length of a 40mm lens.

A flat port also causes peripheral distortion, which leads to blurring and color displacement near the picture edges. This is more obvious when lenses shorter than 35mm are used.

You can take fine photos with a flat-port housing. But don't use a lens shorter than 35mm. We take all our macro photos with our camera in a flat-port housing. It's the right choice for shooting with a 50mm or 100mm macro lens.

A *dome port* compensates for the effect of refraction under water. This means your lenses retain about the same effective focal length under water as they do in air. In addition, edge-to-edge sharpness and color fidelity are retained. Because of these characteristics, dome ports are also named *corrective* ports.

The corrective properties of dome ports make them the logical choice for the serious underwater photographer. You want to work close to your subject under water—in most cases not more than six feet away. This means shooting with a wide-angle lens. When we shoot photos of divers, fish, wrecks or reefs, we use a dome port and a selection of wide-angle lenses ranging from 17mm to 24mm. These lenses let us work close to our subjects—and that's the key to good underwater photography.

When you use a dome port, you must focus on your subject through the viewfinder, as opposed to setting the focus on the distance scale on the lens. Remember, what *you* see under water appears closer than it actually is. However, what the *camera* sees through the dome port does not appear closer than it is, because the port compensates for the underwater foreshortening of distance.

Let's take a specific example: Your underwater subject is eight feet away. To you, it appears

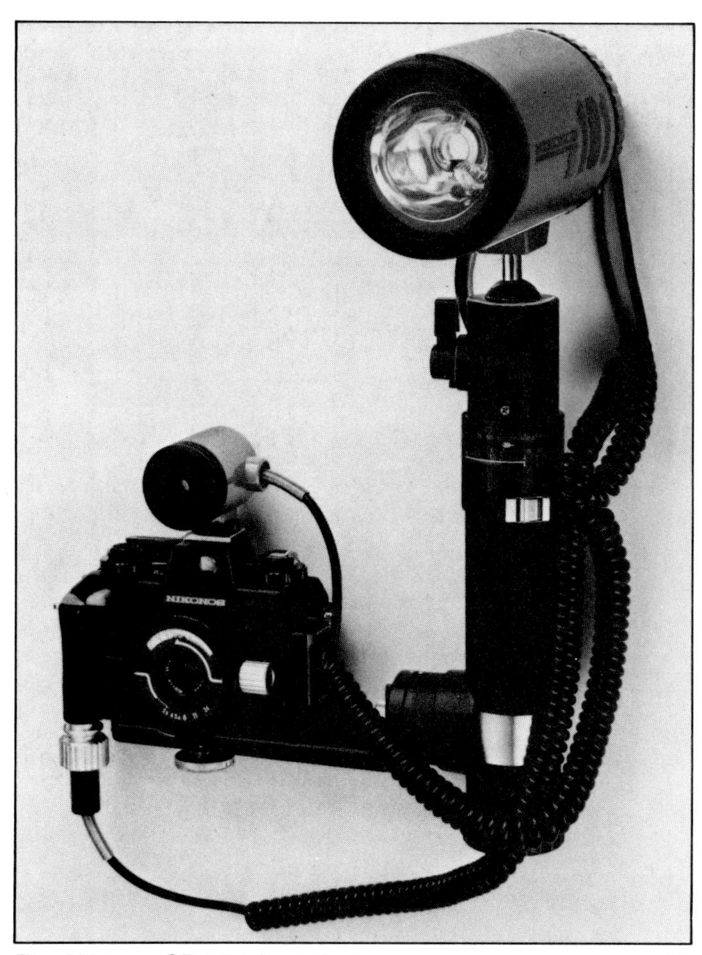

The Nikonos SB-101 flash features an on-camera sensor. It adjusts flash exposure automatically and accurately, no matter how you aim the flash.

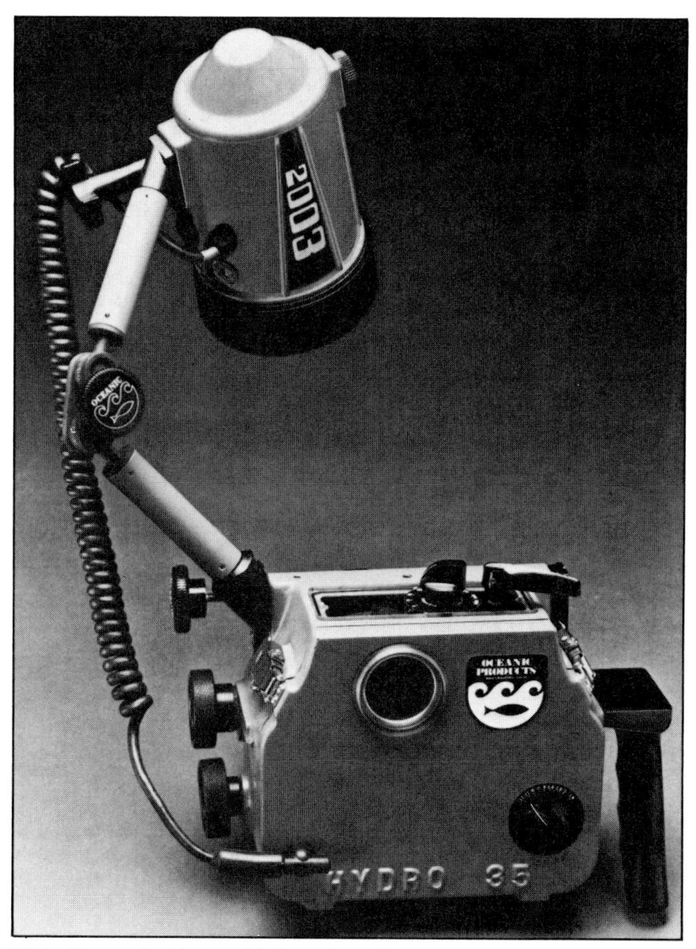

This Oceanic Hydro 35 housing, like most others, has external controls for shutter, lens aperture, focus and film advance. There's also a large viewfinder window and a sturdy hand grip. Flash is important for good underwater photos, so look out for a sturdy flash shoe when you go shopping for a housing.

about six feet away. You set the lens distance scale to six feet. The picture you get is unsharp. Why? Because to the lens behind the dome port the subject was eight feet away!

Before you purchase a dome port, discuss the lenses you plan to use with the housing manufacturer or dealer. He can help you be certain that the lenses and port are compatible.

UNDERWATER ELECTRONIC FLASH

An electronic flash unit is an invaluable accessory for your underwater camera system. You'll want a unit you can handle easily and that delivers consistently well-exposed photos. You'll also want a flash that has a relatively quick recycling time and produces an adequate number of flashes from a single set of batteries.

We discussed the Nikonos SB-101 electronic flash briefly earlier. We also mentioned the Nikonos SB-102 Speedlight. Now we're going to look at underwater flash in general.

There are more than a dozen manufacturers and distributors of underwater electronic-flash units, offering more than 30 different models. It's not easy to select from these, unless you know exactly what you want and need. Let's look at some of the characteristics that are of interest to the underwater photographer.

Before we talk about *submersible* flash units, you should know that several manufacturers of photographic equipment make underwater housings for standard flash units. If you own a flash for your SLR, you can house it for underwater photography. However, these setups have disadvantages. They are awkward to handle under water and the housings have a tendency to float to the surface. Also, with the flash sealed in the housing, you can't make important adjustments such as changing the power setting.

Submersible Electronic Flash— Here's a quick guide to what you should look for when purchasing a flash unit:

- Easy handling is essential. When you're trying to maneuver yourself and your camera into position for the perfect photograph, you want as much freedom of movement as possible. You may want a small, compact flash that is

The Oceanic 2001, 2002 and 2003 electronic flash units. Many other underwater flash units are available. When buying, consider power, ease of handling, angle of coverage and whether a unit has automatic or manual exposure control.

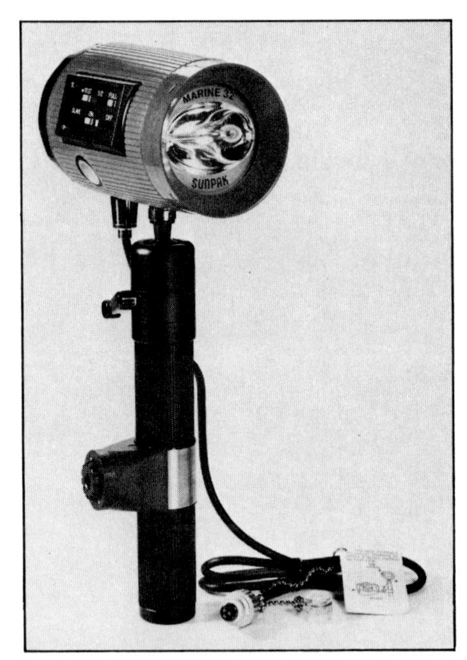

The Sunpak Marine 32 flash can be used on the Nikonos housing and many other housings. It features full-power and half-power settings. It also has a built-in slave sensor, so you can trigger the flash from another unit without cable connection.

negatively buoyant. This eliminates the annoying tendency of the unit trying to rise to the surface of the water.

The Sunpak Marine 32 and Nikonos SB-101 are small units that are easy to handle under water. However, they are not very powerful. Larger, more powerful units, such as the Oceanic 2001 and Ikelite Substrobe 150, are harder to handle. They tend to weigh you down and make it more difficult to swim, especially against a current.

• Arms and trays serve to keep the whole assembly together. A tray holds the camera secure. Arms hold the flash unit or units. A handgrip and light meter are also important to your camera/flash setup. In scuba language, the assembly is called a *rig.* In most cases, the individual items are sold as accessories. You can build your own rig.

The arm should have a *quick-release bracket.* This feature allows you to remove the flash quickly and easily for off-camera illumination.

The tray should have enough holes to enable you to mount the flash, an exposure meter and a handgrip. Your photo dealer may be able to provide you with the exact tray you need. If necessary, you can drill holes and customize a tray yourself. For example, you may want to mount an exposure meter on the side of the tray where there isn't a hole. Or, you may want dual handgrips.

• Choice of exposure mode gives a flash more versatility. Many flash units, including the Sea & Sea Yellow-Sub 50M and the Oceanic 2002, feature automatic and manual exposure control. Some models, such as the Nikonos SB-101, feature two automatic modes plus a variable-power setting, from 1/4 power to full power.

Most of the units we've tried—and we've tried many—work well on the automatic setting. If you're new to underwater photography, we suggest you go with an automatic flash unit.

On automatic, you usually get a larger aperture at a set distance than you would if you were shooting on manual. For example, when the subject is six feet away you may get *f*-4 on automatic and *f*-8 on manual with the same unit. This deprives you of depth of field when you use the automatic setting.

If you choose an automatic flash, make sure that the unit has an on-camera sensor as opposed to a sensor on the flash. This is important when your flash-to-subject distance and direction are different than your camera-to-subject distance and direction.

• Coverage is the angle over which the flash will give uniform illumination. If you want to light a full-frame image, you'll need a flash that covers the angle of view of the widest lens you plan to use with flash. Coverage information is included in the literature that comes with each flash. Read it carefully before you buy. You don't want to end up with a flash that only covers a 35mm lens, if you want to shoot with a 28mm lens.

• A diffuser, placed in front of the flash, will spread the light over a wider area. Diffusers are available for many flash units, including the Nikonos SB-101 and the Sunpak Marine 32. If you start out with a 35mm lens but plan to get a wider lens later, you can buy the narrower-beam flash now and the diffuser later.

The "big guns" in the underwater electronic-flash field are the Oceanic 2001, 2002 and 2003, the Ikelite Substrobe 150 and the Graflex/Subsea Mark 150. All of these are designed to light the scene uniformly, even when you shoot with a 15mm lens.

• Battery power for flash units comes in various forms. If you buy a unit with a built-in rechargeable nickel-cadmium battery, you'll have to be sure it's fully charged before a dive. This is especially important if you're off to some exotic location where you won't find an AC outlet. If you're going to a place where AC power is readily available, bring along your battery charger. However, you may need a voltage converter. Before you leave home, check out the voltage of the place you're visiting.

Many electronic flash units use replaceable batteries— either AA, C or D cells. Before a dive, load your flash with fresh batteries. And take along plenty of extras. You may get to your diving location and find that the last battery there has just been sold!

• The number of flashes you can make with fresh batteries varies from unit to unit and with different batteries. With some flash units, you'll get more than 250 flashes. Others will give you only 80. If you're shooting on automatic, you may get 100 flashes on one diving trip and only 75 on the next. The number varies as the camera-to-subject distances vary. At close range, the flash needs to put out relatively less power. When the subject is farther away, accordingly more power is used.

• A modeling light is a small continuous-light source at virtually the same position as the flash tube. It enables you to evaluate the lighting you'll get from a specific flash position. This feature is rare on portable flash units. However, some brands, such as the Ikelite Substrobe 75 and the Graflex/Subsea Mark 150, do have built-in modeling lights. If you're diving at night or in fairly dark conditions, this light will help you aim the flash.

• A slave sensor lets you fire one flash from another without a cable connection. The Sonic Research SR 2000 and SR 3000, and the Helix Aquaflash 22, have slave sensors. Under water, it's particularly convenient to be able to use two flashes without wires connecting them.

UNDERWATER LIGHT METERS

If you're going to use manual exposure control, either with a Nikonos or a camera in a housing, we recommend that you have an exposure meter. Dives are too costly to rely on exposure estimates.

Three easy-to-read underwater meters are available: Sea & Sea Seameter, Oceanic OM 100 and Sekonic Marine L 164. All are reflected-light, direct-reading meters. You simply point the meter at the subject and take a reading. Then set your camera accordingly. You don't have to line up any needles or make any adjustments.

The Seameter and OM 100 cover an angle of 45°, which is about the angle of view of the Nikonos 35mm lens. The L 164 covers an angle of 30°. We have used all three meters and found each accurate. All three meters can be used to a depth of 160 feet, the maximum recommended depth for sport diving. The meters attach easily to underwater camera housings or camera brackets.

Underwater housings made by Ikelite are available for regular Weston, Gossen and Vivitar meters. However, as with housings for standard electronic flash units, we've found them awkward to handle under water.

EQUIPMENT CARE AND MAINTENANCE

Cameras and photographic accessories need maintenance and tender loving care. In this section, we show you how to avoid problems and costly repairs. We also show you how to deal with flooded equipment.

This Ikelite housing has three hand grips to ensure ease of operation under a wide variety of conditions. On top of each of the two side hand grips is a screw socket for mounting a light meter. A flash or flash extension arm can be attached to the base of each of the side hand grips.

Special light meters are available for the underwater photographer. This Oceanic model, like other underwater meters, ensures good exposures under conditions where the light level would often be difficult to estimate.

If sand gets on your camera, don't try to wipe it off. You are more likely to rub it in. Remove sand, dust and other particles from sensitive camera controls by blowing it away with Dust-Off II or a similar air blower.

CLEANING

No matter what make or model standard or underwater camera you own, proper care and cleaning are important. We recommend the following cleaning procedures:

Camera Body—Examine the camera body, inside and out, before each shooting session. Clean it if necessary—and not otherwise. Excessive cleaning can harm a camera in the long run. However, take note of this story: We have a friend who *never* cleaned his camera. On one occasion, he shot eight rolls of slide film. After processing, each slide had a black line across it. The problem resulted from a hair in the camera, near the film plane. He always inspects the camera now before shooting, and cleans it when necessary.

When you clean the camera interior, don't touch the shutter curtain or the mirror surface, both of which are extremely delicate. The reflective surface on the mirrors in your home is protected by a glass cover. The reflective coating on your SLR mirror is on the front surface and, therefore, unprotected.

Even a fingerprint on the mirror surface is almost impossible to remove. Wiping is bound to damage the mirror. The only particles you should need to remove from the mirror are dust and perhaps occasionally a hair. Brush the mirror *very gently* with a soft antistatic brush.

We find compressed air and small blower brushes effective in removing dust, lint, hairs and even sand from a camera. But don't use compressed air on the shutter curtain and mirror surface. It could damage them. Don't use *excessive* air pressure on *any* camera part.

Dirt on a mirror will not affect the image you get on film. However, it can make viewing and focusing more difficult.

A dirty viewfinder eyepiece can also make focusing difficult. We use a small cotton swab, moistened with lens-cleaning fluid, to get this part of the camera clean.

When necessary, you should also wipe the exterior of the camera to remove grease, dust, suntan lotion and salt spray. We use a silicon-treated camera cloth, available at most camera stores.

Lenses—Always keep the front lens surface free from dirt, dust, fingerprints, salt spray and sand. Never use ordinary household tissue for cleaning a lens. Use only a soft, clean cloth, or lens-cleaning tissue available at camera stores.

For stubborn fingerprints, moisten the cloth or lens-cleaning tissue with photographic lens-cleaning fluid. Gently rub the lens in a circular motion, working from the center to the edges. This motion will remove the marks instead of simply moving them around the lens.

For above-water use, we have a skylight filter on each of our lenses. This filter not only improves color rendition in most outdoor color photographs but also protects the front lens surface.

We always keep the front and rear lens caps on lenses when they are not in use. These caps form a dust-proof container for the lens.

BASIC CARE

Give your camera, its parts and accessories all the care you can. In the long run, it will make your photography more successful, enjoyable and economical.

Battery Care—Under normal circumstances, batteries should provide power to your camera for about one year. During the year, check the battery compartment regularly. If a battery leaks, it can corrode not only the battery compartment but also the inner mechanisms of the camera. If you find a leaking battery, remove it immediately. If you see any indication of contamination by the leak in the battery compartment, have an authorized repairperson check the camera for possible damage.

Here's a simple two-step technique for avoiding battery problems: 1) Change the batteries on your birthday. You'll probably remember that day better than others. This way, you'll always be assured of fresh batteries. Of course, if you take lots of pictures on a regular basis, you may need to change batteries more often. 2) If you're not going to be shooting for more than three or four weeks, remove the batteries and store them separately. Then they can't leak into the battery chamber during the inactive period.

Camera Storage—Moisture can damage the electrical and mechanical parts of your camera. Store your camera in a dry, cool and clean place. It's advisable to store cameras and lenses in plastic bags to protect them from dust, lint, hair and other foreign particles. For additional protection, keep the lens caps on both ends of your lenses.

Insurance—No matter how careful you are, sometimes there are accidents, thefts and losses. We have every piece of photographic equipment we own insured for replacement value. Our insurance agent has a full list of the items, their serial numbers and list prices. In addition, he has b&w photos of the equipment.

Some homeowners' insurance policies cover photographic equipment even when you take it halfway around the world. Others don't. Check with your insurance agent to see how you can fully protect your equipment.

A floating bag not only keeps your accessories dry—it also keeps them afloat. If you're shooting where there is a possibility of something falling in the water, such a bag is a good investment.

KEEP EQUIPMENT SAFE AND DRY

When we are shooting in and around water, we take special precautions to keep cameras, lenses, film, filters and other accessories safe and dry.

On dive boats, a weight belt, tank or other heavy object can easily fall or get dropped. To protect our equipment from such accidents, we keep it in a foam-lined fiberglass case made by Oceanic. These cases are available in several sizes, to fit both large and small camera systems. The cases have rubber seals. They float, even when fully loaded.

Oceanic and Fuji Photo Film U.S.A. also manufacture flexible plastic cases measuring about one-foot square. These cases will keep equipment and film afloat. They are cushioned and feature Velcro seals that keep water out as long as

This photo was taken with a camera that had been flooded at a depth of 45 feet. That's why the image is blurred. You can also see watermarks and other blemishes. Fortunately, the camera was saved. The text tells you how to deal with flooded equipment.

the case is on top of the water. They are not watertight when submerged. We use these cases for boating and rafting trips.

An ordinary plastic sandwich bag, sealed with a wire tie, will also keep film and accessories dry. Just fill the bag up with air, as you would a balloon, and seal it. If the bag should accidentally fall in the water, it will float. However, it may float for only a short time. To prevent your equipment from getting wet or getting lost, retrieve it as quickly as possible.

SAVING FLOODED EQUIPMENT

Your camera may accidentally fall in the water, or your underwater camera or flash may get flooded. You should know how to minimize the need for repair. Here are some procedures we recommend.

If your electronic flash floods, turn it off immediately. Don't touch the wet unit with unprotected hands. If you do, you may get a severe shock. If possible, wear dry gloves of rubber or some other insulating material. Alternatively, turn the unit off with a dry wooden stick or remotely in some other way.

If your camera floods, rewind the film and remove it as quickly as possible. Any part of the film that is reached by the water is likely to be ruined.

If the camera is flooded with salt water, flush it out with clean, fresh water as soon as possible. Salt water will corrode your camera much faster than fresh water.

After flushing the camera out once, soak it in a container full of fresh water for about half an hour. Every five or ten minutes, move the various camera controls. Your objective is to get all the salt out of the camera.

After the fresh-water soak, place the camera in alcohol for one hour. This helps remove all the water from the camera. When you remove it from the alcohol, the camera should dry almost completely by evaporation.

The above are standard procedures recommended by most manufacturers of underwater equipment. However, if you have the opportunity, check beforehand exactly what procedure the manufacturer of the equipment in question recommends.

The final step is perhaps the most important: Get the piece of equipment to a repair shop as quickly as possible. Give the repairperson all the details about the flooding and the steps you took to save the item.

Use of a telephoto lens helped in several ways for this picture. It enabled us to "get close" to the birds. It also made the bridge appear larger and more prominent. The limited depth of field also put the bridge a little out of focus, keeping the main attention on the birds.

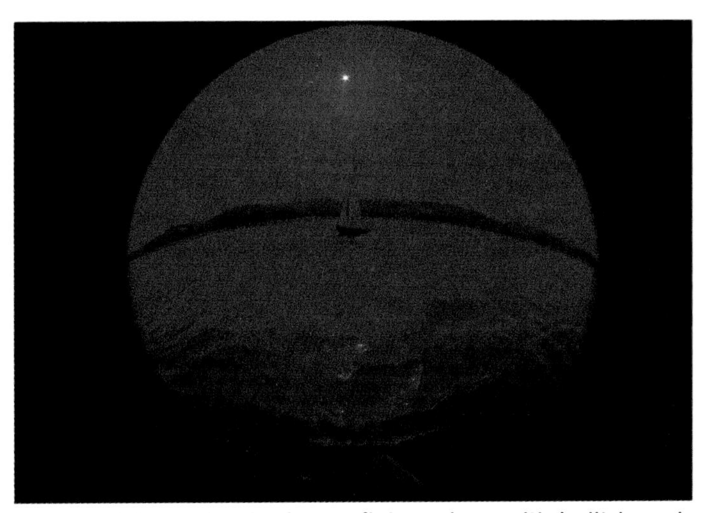

Using a 7.5mm circular-image fisheye lens with built-in red filter enabled us to produce this unusual image.

With a full-frame fisheye lens, you can create surrealistic images like this. When you place the horizon near the picture edge, it records with a curvature. Had the horizon been placed in the lower half of the frame, it would have curved in the other direction. Straight lines passing through the center of the frame are the only ones that record straight.

The subject need not always fill the image area. This picture is effective because it conveys how the subject feels—surrounded by lots of cool water. Climb onto a diving board, use a wide-angle lens, and be sure the sun is in the right position to add shimmering highlights to the water. Photo by Lou Jones.

2 Underwater Photography

Good underwater photography requires the appropriate equipment, a little experience and lots of patience. Satisfy these three requirements, and you can bring home precious memories of your diving experiences. And you can share them with those less intrepid than you.

If you have ever seen an episode of *The Undersea World of Jacques Cousteau* or a feature in *National Geographic* magazine on coral reefs, you are aware of the fantastic beauty that lies in the oceans. Colorful fish, exotic plants and strange coral "cities" make the ocean realm a fascinating place to see and photograph.

Sophisticated *self-contained underwater breathing apparatus* (*SCUBA* gear) makes visiting this underwater world possible. A face mask gives you a clear view of underwater life. Air tanks and regulators let you breathe easily. A wet or dry suit keeps you comfortable. Fins give you mobility. And buoyancy compensators make you virtually weightless.

LEARN TO DIVE

Each year, hundreds of thousands of people enjoy scuba diving. The YMCA offers a ten-week certificate course in diving. We've taken this course and found it extremely helpful. Local divers' equipment and supply shops (dive shops) can tell you who gives scuba instruction in your area. Also see the *Yellow Pages,* under *Diving.* Courses usually include classroom lectures, swimming-pool sessions and open-water dives.

A certificate, or "C card," is proof of your experience. The card, awarded on completion of a course, proves you are familiar with basic scuba equipment and safety. Most dive shops in the U.S.A., Mexico and the Caribbean will only do business with people who have C cards. They don't want to endanger themselves or other divers. So, if you want to rent equipment or get on a dive boat, get your C card first.

Many vacation spots in the Caribbean and on the coast of Mexico provide a one-day scuba-diving course. You'll learn the basics there. However, we recommend that you take a more comprehensive course at home.

For many, being on the water surface is not enough. They are drawn to explore the underwater world. When they've experienced its fascination, they are likely to go back again and again. And they will want to photograph what they see. Diving on a shipwreck or coral reef is a fantastic visual experience. In this scene, visibility was about 100 feet. Susan, who's in the picture, had a clear view of the wreck and the fish. Good visibility also helped Rick get a sharp and clear picture.

Undaunted by cumbersome camera equipment and slow film emulsions, Louis Boutan of France made this photo in 1899. It is one of the earliest underwater photographs.

ENVIRONMENT

Coral cities are inhabited by many different kinds of marine life. In one square yard you may find brain coral, feather-duster worms, sea fans, tube sponges, sea urchins, starfish, crabs, parrotfish, stonefish and more. Away from the coral reef, you'll see larger fish, such as jackfish, stingrays and manta rays.

These colorful and often strangely shaped sea creatures are interesting to observe and fun to photograph. However, shooting through water is different than shooting in air, as you will soon see.

VISIBILITY

Scuba diving is a fantastic visual experience. That's why divers are prepared to travel to distant diving areas that offer the best visibility.

Resorts in the Caribbean boast of "crystal-clear water with visibility beyond 100 feet." In Belize, Central America, the dive shops claim that visibility is "always 150 feet." In the Philippines, visibility is described as a "guaranteed 200 feet." The quoted visibilities are at depths to about 30 feet. Obviously, this extensive visibility is great for photographing under water.

We have dived at all of the above locations over the past five years. More often than not, visibility was good. Our dives were on bright, sunny days, with no wind or clouds. We've also had our share of disappointing dives, when visibility was less than half of what we had anticipated. These dives were on days that were cloudy, windy or rainy.

Good visibility is a relative term. As residents of New York, we are used to visibility of about 10 feet in our local waters. When we can see over 40 feet, we're thrilled. Florida residents, who frequent the Keys, think that visibility of 60 feet is good.

BEST TIME TO DIVE

The best time to dive is between 10 a.m. and 2 p.m. During these hours, sunlight has to penetrate the least amount of water because the sun is relatively high in the sky. Therefore, it's brighter down below. In the early-morning and late-afternoon hours, when the sun is very low, more sunlight is reflected off the surface, with less light illuminating the underwater world. This reduces visibility.

Noon is the ideal time to dive. If possible, try to schedule your dive so that you are in the water at that time.

WEATHER CONDITIONS

Weather conditions also affect how much you'll be able to see and photograph under water. If it's windy and the water is choppy, much of the light is lost by scattered reflection from the surface. Because less light penetrates the water, visibility and maximum shooting distance, as well as subject contrast, are decreased. Wind also stirs up particles in the water, reducing visibility.

Overcast and cloudy skies also affect what you'll be able to see and photograph. For example, on a sunny day visibility may be 100 feet at noon. A completely overcast sky can reduce this to 30 or 40 feet.

Before you make arrangements for a dive, check the weather conditions, or in scuba talk, the *reef report.* If the report is bad, it may be better to relax around the hotel or local town until the wind dies down and the sun comes out.

SUBJECT SIZE

Light rays behave differently in media of different *densities.* In water, which is denser than air, objects will appear nearer and larger than they would at the same distance in air. If you've ever stood in a swimming pool and looked down at your strangely short-looking legs, you have experienced this effect. Your feet suddenly seem *larger* and *closer* to your eyes. It's due to the *refraction* of light.

You can also see how refraction affects subject size in your kitchen. Drop a spoon into a glass of water. The half in the water will look larger (or closer) than the top half.

The apparent change in subject

size caused by refraction can lead to focusing errors. Refraction causes objects to look about 25% closer underwater than they actually are. For example, if a subject is actually about eight feet away from you, it will appear to be about six feet away.

If you are focusing through the lens of a 35mm SLR, this difference won't bother you. What you see in the viewfinder is what you get on the film. However, if you are setting focus on the distance scale of a lens, set it for the distance you *see*. In the above example, don't set the lens to the eight feet at which you *know* the subject to be. Set it to the six feet at which you *see* the subject.

COLOR LOSS

One of the biggest disappointments to the beginning underwater photographer is the absence of color in his photographs. He sees and photographs purple sea fans, green sponges, pink sweepers, orange coral and yellowtail fish. When he sees his pictures, he wonders where the colors have gone and why his photos look blue.

The answer to this perplexing question is simple. Water filters out colors selectively. The deeper you dive, the more colors you lose from the sunlight that's illuminating the scene. In clear water, color penetrates more deeply than in murky water.

The red component of the light starts to go first. In clear water, it

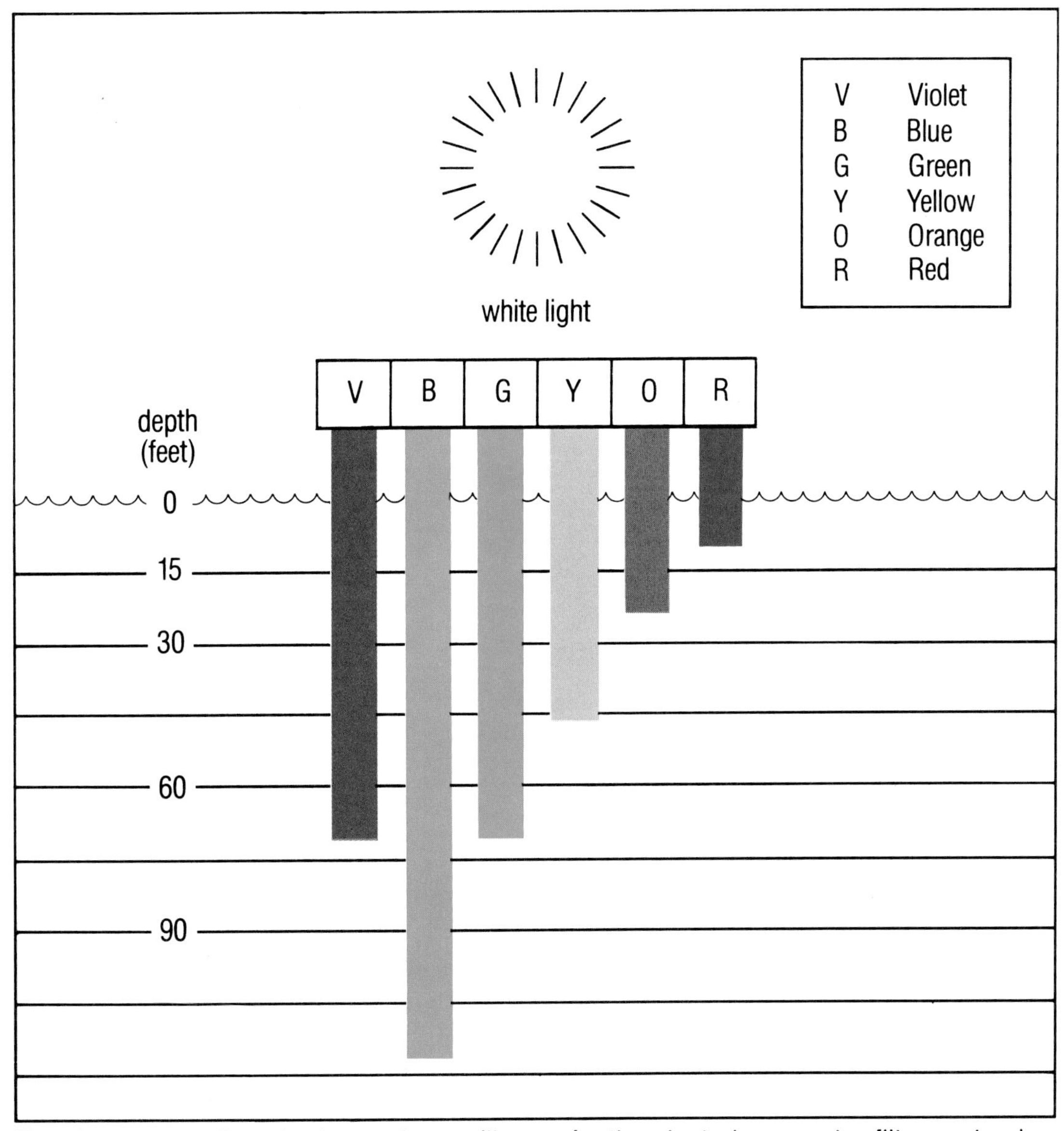

The deeper you dive, the less color you'll see. As the chart shows, water filters out colors selectively. As you go deeper, red and orange go first, followed by yellow. Blue penetrates to the greatest depth. That's why photos taken in deep water have a characteristic blue appearance. You can avoid this color loss by taking a flash unit and using it close to the subject.

This chart is only an approximate guide. Precise distances depend on the clarity of the water and on weather conditions. Also, the color penetration does not end abruptly, as would appear from the chart. It decreases gradually.

The jellyfish was photographed by daylight at a depth of about 50 feet. Under these conditions, you'll need high-speed film. We used Ektachrome 200. For a delicate subject like this, it's important to have a plain, unobtrusive background.

is completely filtered out at approximately 13 feet. Orange is completely filtered out at about 18 feet. Yellow goes at 45 feet.

The chart on the previous page shows how the different colors of the spectrum are filtered out at different depths in clear water.

False Color—Why does a diver still see reds, yellows, purples and a wealth of other colors, at depths where we know they are filtered out? It's because his eyes and brain play tricks on him under water.

For example, if you are diving with a buddy whom you *know* to be wearing a red wet suit, you'll *see* the red suit—perhaps even at 40 feet. Your brain knows it's red, so you see it as red. The film, however, doesn't *know* the suit is red and records it as blue. If you recognize a yellowtail fish from a close-up flash photo you've seen in a book, you will *see* the yellow tail, even in 50 feet of water by available light. In reality, the color is filtered out, so you don't see any yellow. Therefore, if you have no previous knowledge of the tail being yellow, it'll appear bluish.

The above is, of course, an oversimplification of the very complex topic of subjective vision. However, it makes a pertinent point.

The way to record colors accurately under water is to use flash close to the subject. Remember, the closer the *light source* is to the subject, the less colors are filtered out by the water.

EQUIPMENT AND FILM

To record your underwater adventures, there is a wide variety of cameras, lenses and accessories from which you can choose. Chapter 1 helped you select the equipment that would best suit your water-photography requirements. Here, we would like to add a few words specifically to the *underwater* photographer.

SETTING UP

Always be sure that all your camera gear is set up and ready for use before you leave shore. Cameras should be loaded and properly adjusted. A camera sealed in a housing should be ready for use. The motor drive or auto winder should also be switched on.

If you're not ready to take the plunge as soon as your boat drops anchor, you may spend 15 valuable minutes loading film, checking camera settings and making sure the gear is properly sealed. This way, you lose valuable diving time. Also, if the boat is bobbing up and down, they could be an uncomfortable 15 minutes.

Safe Entry—Never dive into the water with your camera in hand. It could get damaged or it could hurt you by smashing you in the face.

Sometimes you encounter extreme contrast under water. Here, we exposed the film to maintain color and detail in the sunlit fish. Fortunately, the slide film's useful exposure range was great enough to also record some detail in the deep shadows.

Or, you could drop it and see it sink or float away. You also need both hands free when you first get into the water.

When you have dived into the water, first check out your diving gear. When you feel comfortable in the water, swim back to the boat and have someone hand you your camera.

FILM

You use basically the same films underwater as in your photography on dry land. We don't think it's necessary to provide you with a list of what's available. However, we would like to give some specific recommendations to the underwater photographer.

Start with Fast Film—Whether you want color slides, color prints or b&w prints, it's advisable to use a fast film on your first few dives. Films in the ISO 400/27° to ISO 1000/31° range offer two advantages over slower films. You can shoot at a faster shutter speed, to stop more movement in available-light photography. You can also shoot at a smaller *f*-stop, to get more depth of field. This allows you some margin for error in focusing or distance estimating.

We recommend the fast-shutter-speed/small-aperture combination until you get used to shooting in the underwater environment. Eventually, you'll want to be selective with aperture and shutter-speed settings. At times you may want a large aperture for selective focus on a specific subject part. Sometimes you'll want to shoot at a slow shutter speed to intentionally blur the image.

Grain—Fast films have relatively coarse grain, visible in projected slides and enlargements. When you have some underwater experience and want images with fine grain, shoot with a slower film. Kodachrome 64, for example, has virtually no visible grain. The faster Ektachrome 200 will also give you good results although grain is evident in large projected images and enlargements. For crisp b&w prints without noticeable grain, we use ISO 125/22° Kodak Plus-X film.

Forgiving Film—Some films offer exposure latitude that "forgives" your errors. When we first started taking underwater pictures, we used Kodacolor 400 color-print film extensively. We found it a great film to learn with because we

B&W film is often ideal for underwater photography. When the subject is relatively colorless and prevailing conditions filter out what color there might be, we use b&w film. This photo was taken by daylight in 50 feet of water on Kodak Tri-X film. We found this scene at John Penneykamp National Park in Key Largo, Florida.

Because objects look closer under water than on land, wide-angle lenses are especially valuable. Both of these photographs were taken with a 17mm lens, which we use frequently. It allows us to come very close to our subjects—a key to good underwater photography. The camera was in an underwater housing.

could overexpose it by a step or two and still produce acceptable prints.

Now, we use Kodachrome 64 color-slide film most of the time for daylight and electronic-flash shooting. We prefer the beautiful color reproduction and fine grain of this film over any film we have tried.

Deep Diving—At a depth greater than 50 feet, light is scarce even in clear water on a sunny day. For natural-light photos under those conditions, we'll use Ektachrome 200. It is more than 1-1/2 times as fast as Kodachrome 64.

Slide or Print—We now shoot slide film almost exclusively because underwater scenes look terrific projected on the home screen. When we want a print from a slide, we just send it to our friendly local photo lab. With the slide as a reference, making a matching print is easy. With negative film, we've found that color balance tends to vary from lab to lab and print to print.

LENSES

The key to good underwater photography is to get as close to the subject as possible—whatever lens is used. Plankton, foreign particles and turbulence all reduce visibility and image quality. Therefore, the less water you have between the camera and your subject, the sharper and clearer your photographs will be.

Fisheye Lens—These lenses are not for realistic images. They can, however, produce grossly distorted images that can be very effective. Depth of field is virtually unlimited. Fisheye lenses of 6mm to 10mm focal length produce a circular image in the 35mm frame.

Wide-Angle Lens—Lenses in the 15mm to 28mm focal-length range allow you to work close to divers, medium-size fish and coral heads and still get the whole subject in the picture. They also offer extensive depth of field.

Medium-Wide-Angle and Standard Lens—These lenses, in the 35mm to 50mm range, are suitable for photographing creatures you don't want to approach too closely—such as the relatives of *Jaws!*

Telephoto Lens—There is little use for these lenses under water. If you try to photograph something more than 15 or 20 feet away, the density of the water will render it blue. Image sharpness will also be poor.

Macro Lens—To capture the beauty, color and detail of a coral reef close-up, the macro lens is ideal. Many divers prize their macro or close-up photos most of all.

Effective Focal Length—Effective focal length is an important thing to consider when choosing a lens. Think about what kind of pictures you want to take before you jump in the water. Remember, you can't change lenses below the surface.

You know by now that *effective* focal length refers specifically to underwater use, where objects look closer than they actually are. This makes a 35mm lens behave underwater as if it had a focal length of about 50mm. An 80mm lens will behave as if its focal length were about 100mm.

Bear all this in mind when you choose a lens. But remember also that it applies *only* to lenses used behind a *flat* port. A *dome* port compensates for the underwater compression of distance. And so do the dome-port Nikonos 15mm and 28mm lenses.

SHOOTING BY DAYLIGHT

For your first few underwater photo sessions, it's best to shoot in daylight. This will allow you to concentrate all your attention on selecting your subject and composing the scene. Shooting with electronic flash is a little more tricky. It is covered in the next section of this chapter.

Composing a scene underwater is not as easy as it sounds. Fish, divers and marine plants are usually all moving at the same time, often in different directions. The less equipment you have to think about, the better off you are.

MAXIMUM SHOOTING DISTANCE

The practical maximum camera-to-subject distance for daylight photography is limited to about 25% of visibility. This is because film is less sensitive than the eye and cannot adapt to dim light as the eye can. If visibility is 100 feet, maximum shooting distance is about 25-35 feet. When visibility is 50 feet, you can shoot to a distance of about 12-15 feet.

Don't be deceived by the fact that objects look nice and clear well beyond the recommended shooting distance. On a photograph, they won't look that good. The image is likely to have poor definition. Also, exposures will tend to be long.

Being restricted to shooting close to your subject is not as much of a limitation as you may think. With a 15mm Nikonos lens or a 17mm lens in a dome-port housing, you can photograph a diver full-length from about eight feet away. With wide-angle lenses in the 20mm to 35mm range, you can get great shots of fish from two or three feet away. Shooting as close as possible to your subject is one of the keys to getting good underwater photos.

This underwater scene was illuminated by sunlight. The shipwreck lay at a depth of 50 feet. Visibility was about 80 feet. Rick shot from 20 feet away, getting a clear and dramatic photo.

To create a feeling of motion, you can *pan* the camera under water just as you do on land. Panning involves using a relatively slow shutter speed and swinging the camera in unison with the moving object during exposure. This results in a sharp subject against a blurred background. You often see the same effect in motor racing photos, where the background of spectators is recorded as a horizontal blur. This photo was made with a shutter speed of 1/30 second. The technique worked here, even though there were many fish, because the fish swam in unison.

UNDERWATER EXPOSURE GUIDE

The figures in this chart are based on crystal-clear water, sunny day, shooting time between 10 a.m. and 2 p.m. and camera-to-subject distance of not more than eight feet. The exposures recommended are approximate and can vary with slight changes in the prevailing conditions.

The figures below are based on an exposure time of 1/125 second.

	Film Speed		
Depth (feet)	**ISO 64/19° Aperture**	**ISO 200/24° Aperture**	**ISO 400/27° Aperture**
5	*f*-8	*f*-11 to *f*-16	*f*-16 to *f*-22
10	*f*-5.6	*f*-8 to *f*-11	*f*-11 to *f*-16
20	*f*-4	*f*-5.6 to *f*-8	*f*-8 to *f*-11
30	*f*-2.8	*f*-4 to *f*-5.6	*f*-5.6 to *f*-8
40	*f*-2	*f*-2.8 to *f*-4	*f*-4 to *f*-5.6
50		*f*-2 to *f*-2.8	*f*-2.8 to *f*-4
60			*f*-2 to *f*-2.8

GETTING GOOD COLOR

As we discussed earlier in this chapter, water filters out different colors at different depths. There are three techniques you can use to get better color in natural-light photographs:

- Dive in shallow water. Colors are most intense at depths less than 20 or 30 feet. Incidentally, you'll also find most of the fish and other marine life there.
- Shoot close. Color is filtered out by the water horizontally as well as vertically. Therefore, the closer your subject, the more color you'll get.
- Use a filter. Using an amber or red filter on the camera lens will reduce the bluish cast the image would otherwise have. You can try a CC30R filter or a yellowish 81A or 81B to *warm up* the image. Filters are useless, however, if you're at a depth of more than 15 feet. At that depth, there will be no red left in the light, and no amount of filtration will bring it back.

Underwater Filters—These specially designed filters have small holes in the filter rings to let water in between filter and lens. This lets you mount and remove a filter under water. If air were trapped in the space between filter and lens, the water pressure on the filter would prevent you from removing the filter.

The tiny holes can cause problems, if you're not careful. If you jump into the water with a filter on and start shooting immediately, water may not completely have filled the air space, so part of your photo will be blurred. Check to see that there are no air bubbles between filter and lens before you start shooting.

EXPOSURE

Thanks to automatic-exposure cameras, getting well-exposed underwater photos in natural light is relatively easy. You simply aim the camera, focus and shoot. Chances are that exposures will be pretty good. With a manual camera, you can determine correct exposure with an underwater light meter.

To ensure well-exposed pictures, bracket your exposures. Make at least two additional exposures of each subject. One should be one *f*-stop (or exposure step) over the recommended setting and the other one stop under.

Shutter Speeds—To "freeze" on film the movement of an average fish that doesn't swim particularly fast, shoot at a shutter speed of 1/125 second or faster. Divers moving at a leisurely, slow speed should also be photographed within this shutter-speed range.

You can use a shutter speed of 1/60 second or 1/30 second to create the feeling of motion in a photograph. For example, if you want to blur the background and have the subject sharp, as in the picture on the opposite page, you can use the *panning* technique. First select and set a slow shutter speed. When the subject swims past you, swing the camera to follow the motion in the viewfinder. When the subject is in the best position for a picture, shoot. Continue to swing the camera to follow the subject for a second after exposure. This will ensure a smooth pan. The resulting photo should show the subject reasonably sharp against a streaked background.

Lens Aperture—The *f*-stop you use for correct exposure is determined by the shutter speed, or vice versa. The smaller the aperture, the more depth of field you'll have—and the slower a shutter speed you must use.

Exposure Chart—The accompanying chart shows *f*-stop/shutter-speed combinations for ISO 64/19°, ISO 200/24° and ISO 400/27° film at various water depths. The chart is based on crystal-clear water, a time between 10 a.m. and 2 p.m. and a clear, sunny day. As you see, the light approximately halves with every additional 10 feet of depth.

If the conditions are windy, cloudy or overcast, or if you're shooting early or late in the day, you'll have to increase exposure. Water clarity also affects exposure. With all these variables, you can understand why it's great to have an automatic camera or hand-held meter. They can save you a lot of calculations.

UNUSUAL LIGHTING

Under water, as on land, in-camera and hand-held exposure meters can occasionally be "fooled" into giving you an incorrect reading. For example, you may be shooting downward toward a coral head that is surrounded by sand. The meter will compensate for the light reflected from the bright sand and thus underexpose the darker coral head. In a case like this, you should

PEOPLE PICTURES

Making good underwater photos of divers demands a keen eye and coordination between diver and photographer. Here are a few tips that will help you get beautiful shots of your underwater companion:

Avoid Awkwardness

In the underwater environment, where you can achieve apparent weightlessness, legs and arms tend to move awkwardly. First-time divers often look pretty silly trying to remain stationary under water.

Discuss the position you want your buddy to assume *before* you dive. He can then position himself accordingly—and as gracefully as possible—for your underwater portraits.

If you are diving on a shipwreck, have your companion grasp the ship's railing. With something to hold on to, he can control his movement much more easily.

Action Photos

It's fun to photograph divers in action. Have your buddy chase a fish toward you or photograph him as he swims over a coral head. You can also make interesting photos of a diver swimming through an underwater tunnel or into a coral cavern. Of course, you must use flash.

Diving Equipment

Snorkels, weight belts and air hoses shift position under water. When you are composing a shot, make sure there isn't an air hose "growing out of a diver's head" or a snorkel "sticking out of his ear!"

Air Bubbles

Air bubbles from a regulator can add the effect of motion to a photo of a diver. Observe the breathing rhythm of your subject and shoot just after he has let out a breath of air.

Mouthpiece

A diver doesn't generally look very flattering with an air-regulator mouthpiece distorting his lips and cheeks. To avoid showing this, photograph your companion from slightly off to one side. If you shoot him head-on, have him tilt his head up or down a little so the mouthpiece cover hides the unflattering parts.

move close to the coral head to ensure getting a meter reading of it alone. If you shoot downward at divers and fish, you may underexpose them for the same reason unless you take a close-up reading.

Silhouettes—Dramatic silhouettes of divers, boats and schools of fish are easy to take. Point the camera upward and frame your subject between you and the sun. If you are shooting with an automatic camera, the meter will read the bright part of the scene and expose for it. The main subject will be silhouetted. With a manual camera, take a reading of the highlight areas and expose for them.

Silhouettes seem to capture the special beauty and tranquility of diving. On our dives, we always make a point of shooting a couple of silhouettes.

The beauty and drama of diving is recorded particularly effectively in silhouette. At left is our original image. The camera was aimed upward, toward the water surface and the sun. The two other images were generated from the first by laser enhancement. This service is provided by LaserColor Labs of West Palm Beach, Florida.

FLASH PHOTOGRAPHY

Shooting with electronic flash adds a whole new dimension to underwater photography. Because the light source is close to the subject, colors come alive—sometimes even those that are invisible to the eye. Shadows in coral reefs and divers' face masks are filled with light and detail. If you shoot a mask head-on, however, you'll get a detail-killing reflection from the port. Avoid shooting at masks head-on when using on-camera flash.

With flash, depth of field can be increased and fast-moving subjects can be "frozen" in position. However, using electronic flash under water—even an automatic unit—requires practice.

CHOOSING A FLASH

For below the water as above water, there are two basic types of electronic flash units. Automatic models adjust the flash output automatically as the flash-to-subject distance changes. You set the *f*-stop on the camera lens once and the flash delivers the proper amount of light for good exposure. With manual flash units, you have to adjust the *f*-stop every time the flash-to-subject distance changes.

Some flash units feature two automatic modes plus manual operation. There are even units that have *modeling lights,* so you can see where your flash is aimed. *Slave cells* that enable you to fire one flash from another without connecting cables are also available.

In Chapter 1 we introduced you to some flash equipment suitable for underwater use. Choose a unit that best fills your specific shooting requirements.

ANGLE OF COVERAGE

Generally, the coverage angle of your electronic flash should match or exceed the angle of coverage of the lens you're shooting with. If the angle of the flash is wider than that of the lens, your flash positioning doesn't need to be perfect. That can be a definite help, especially under water. If the flash beam is narrower than the angle of view of the lens, only the central part of the subject may be illuminated.

Normally, a wide-beam flash should be used with 16mm to

28mm wide-angle lenses. A narrow-beam unit should be used with semi-wide and standard lenses of 35mm to 50mm.

For the one-flash owner, a wide-beam unit may be the best choice because it can be used with all lenses. However, if you think that you will be photographing with the standard lens only, go with a narrow beam unit. It has the advantage of being less expensive and less cumbersome. Also, the narrower the beam, the more concentrated the light.

If you consistently use a wide-beam flash with a lens of narrower angle, you waste a lot of the light. By concentrating the light only into the area that needs to be lit, you get maximum illumination in the scene.

EXPOSURE

A perfectly exposed underwater flash picture "pops" with color and detail. It's worth taking all possible care to ensure accurate exposure.

Manual Operation—The light output of a flash is expressed by a *guide number* for a specific film speed. This guide number helps you determine the correct *f*-stop at a certain flash-to-subject distance. When shooting in air, you divide the guide number by the flash-to-subject distance to get the *f*-number for acceptable exposure.

Here's a basic rule for underwater photography: In crystal-clear water, use the in-air guide number recommended by the manufacturer of the flash. Then open the aperture by one *f*-stop beyond the one indicated by that guide number.

For example, if the regular guide number is 50 (feet) and the flash-to-subject distance is five feet, the recommended aperture would be almost exactly *f*-11. In very clear water, you would set the aperture at *f*-8.

When you're doing your calculations, be sure to use the *flash-to-subject* distance. It may sometimes differ from the *camera-to-subject* distance.

Water Clarity—The amount of light reaching the subject is affected by water clarity. Particles in the water not only reduce visibility, they also cut down the amount of illumination the flash provides at a specific distance. In unclear water, you'll have to reduce the guide number accordingly. This means you'll have to shoot at a larger aperture.

As the flash-to-subject distance increases in water that's less than crystal-clear, you'll have to make two adjustments. First, you must reduce the recommended guide

CATCH A FISH

Here are some tips on how to get sharp, full-frame and well-composed photos of fleeting fish:

Be Patient

Most fish will be frightened away when you plunge into the water. However, once you settle down and stop adjusting all your diving and photo gear, you'll see the fish returning to their "home turf." Fish are very territorial, and it takes more than a diver or two to keep them away from their feeding place for long.

Don't start shooting the moment you get into the water. If you do, you'll get nothing but photos of fishtails! Let the fish swim away and then wait for their return. Then you'll have a chance to shoot away to your heart's content.

Feeding

Fish love to eat—constantly. Chopped-up hot dogs, cheese and bread are among the many snacks that are always acceptable. When they see or sense food, they'll come swimming fast.

Plastic film containers are ideal for taking fish food under water. You can have an entire school of fish eating out of your hand—literally!

For convincing photos of fish in their natural environment, hide a food container on a coral head, out of the camera's view. For a really interesting shot, ask your diving buddy to feed the fish.

Caution

Don't take any dead fish or other sea creatures under water as food. They could attract larger and unwelcome creatures that may find you appetizing, too.

Preset Exposure and Focus

If you preset focus and lens aperture before you dive, all you have to do under water is frame the subject at the right distance, position your flash and shoot. This makes it easier to capture fast-moving subjects that don't like to pose.

Dive at Night

When the sun goes down, fish head for nooks and crannies that offer protection from night predators. When the fish are asleep, you can get to within a few inches of them and make great close-ups. The flash doesn't seem to disturb them.

Of course, you'll need a diving companion with an underwater light to guide you on your underwater adventure.

When you take commonsense precautions, you needn't be afraid to dive at night. Local guides and dive operators at most diving locations know where the safe spots are. In Key Largo, Florida, for example, there is no record of a diver ever being hurt on a night dive.

Fish love to eat. This photo was taken a few seconds after Susan had opened a can filled with bread. So many fish had gathered in this time that Susan is almost invisible behind all the fish. If you look carefully, you can see one of her legs.

An orange clown fish passing by a green sea anemone makes a colorful picture. The scene was shot by sunlight at a water depth of about eight feet. The same scene at a depth of 30 feet would look all blue—unless it were lit by a nearby flash.

number to compensate for the murkiness of the water. Second, you must divide that new guide number by the new shooting distance, to get the correct *f*-number setting.

Clear and *unclear* are relative terms. Therefore, compensation for water murkiness can only be approximate. Whenever possible, bracket exposures.

Automatic Operation—Automatic flash units take practically all the guesswork out of flash exposure. On-camera sensors measure the light reflected from the subject and adjust exposure accordingly. You don't need to get involved in time-consuming calculations each time you change the flash-to-subject distance. You just set the aperture once, point your camera at the subject, focus and shoot.

Most automatic flash units offer two auto settings. One gives you an aperture for shooting from, say, six inches to about eight feet. The other may give you an aperture for a distance range of, say, six inches to 12 feet.

At the closer maximum shooting distance—eight feet in the above example—you'll have a smaller *f*-stop. This gives you more depth of field. The aperture for the greater maximum shooting distance is usually considerably larger—about two or three stops.

Select the power setting that will give you the depth of field you want for a particular shot.

Remember that water murkiness cuts down the effectiveness of the light. Therefore, in unclear water, the advertised maximum shooting distance is reduced considerably.

MIXING FLASH WITH DAYLIGHT

The most natural-looking underwater photographs are those made with a mixture of flash and daylight. When properly balanced, this kind of lighting reduces or eliminates harsh shadows. The result is a photograph with color and detail, but lacking that artificial head-on-flash look.

Balance the Lights—Mixing the two light sources is relatively easy with an in-camera or handheld meter with *f*-stop and shutter-speed readouts. Following is a step-by-step method for determining correct exposure when combining daylight and flash:

Meter the scene for daylight exposure. Let's assume you're shooting Kodachrome 64 at a depth of 10 feet in clear water under a noontime sun. The exposure-meter reading should be about 1/60 second at *f*-8.

Calculate the *f*-stop for the flash-to-subject distance, as described earlier in this chapter. If the aperture setting is smaller than the one for daylight—say, *f*-11 in our example—set the smaller aperture on your lens. The nearby subject will be properly exposed. The background will be slightly dark, adding to the underwater effect.

If you used the daylight setting, the flash would overexpose the nearby subject. This would give you a washed-out and colorless slide or too dense a negative image.

If the *f*-stop for the flash exposure is larger than that for the daylight exposure, use the daylight setting. The area of the subject illuminated by sunlight will be correctly exposed. To minimize underexposure of the subject, come closer if you possibly can. Alternatively, remove the flash from the camera and hold it as close to the subject as possible. Be careful not to get the flash unit into the picture.

If you used the larger aperture setting, the background would be overexposed. It would be washed-out in a slide and would tend to be too dense in a negative.

The most impressive underwater illumination often consists of a balanced mixture of flash and daylight. Without flash, the diver would have been in silhouette and much of the foreground detail lost. Without daylight, the bright-blue water background would have been a dull black.

Optimum Control—You *can* get *precise* control of the flash-to-daylight balance in one of three ways:

1) Change the flash-to-subject distance. To give you sufficient control under varying conditions, you may need an extra-long cord for your flash. You'll probably also need an assistant to hold the flash for you.

2) Change the shutter speed. A shutter speed of 1/30 second will give you twice the background exposure you'll get with a 1/60 second. This change in the shutter setting will have no effect on the flash exposure. A shutter speed of 1/125 second will halve the background exposure without affecting the flash exposure.

However, be sure to use a shutter speed that synchronizes properly with the flash.

All SLR focal-plane shutters synchronize at 1/60 second and slower. Some also sync at 1/125 second. At least one camera's shutter even syncs at 1/250 second. See your camera manual for details. Blade shutters synchronize at all speeds.

3) Change the power output. A variable power output is very useful for flash-and-daylight photography. If you plan to do this kind of photography regularly, you should have a flash unit that offers this feature.

For additional general information on mixing light sources, see *How to Select and Use Electronic Flash,* also published by HPBooks.

BACKSCATTER

One of the biggest problems you'll encounter when shooting with flash under water is *backscatter.* It is unwanted light that is scattered, or bounced off, particles in the water. These tiny obstacles—sand, plankton and sometimes air bubbles—are not always readily visible to the eye. However, the strong and directional light of the flash is reflected by them. The result is an image in which it is apparently snowing.

The backscatter effect is most prominent when the flash is positioned on or close to the camera. This is because the light is reflected straight back into the lens.

You can reduce, or even eliminate, backscatter by holding the flash off camera at arm's length. The light will still bounce off the particles, but most of it will bounce back toward the flash and not to the camera. Most underwater flash units are equipped with a quick-release bracket or ball-joint arm that lets you position the flash away from the camera.

We take most of our flash pictures with off-camera flash. During our early underwater adventures, we spoiled many otherwise excellent photos with backscatter. We don't take chances any more!

AIMING THE FLASH

Although holding the flash away from the camera is generally no problem, aiming it accurately can be. Imagine that you're diving with your new flash for the first time. You see a beautiful queen angel fish. You detach your flash

SCUBA SAFETY

Although you'll be concentrating on taking great photos, your *prime* concern should be *safety.* Here are a few basic rules for safe diving with your camera:

Plan Your Dive and Dive Your Plan

Always plan your dive in advance and, when possible, stick to that plan throughout the dive. This avoids confusion under water and makes it easier for you to get the photos you want.

Obviously you can't plan every single move in advance. If you did, you would be so limited that you would not get any worthwhile pictures. But a *basic* plan of action is essential. What is equally essential is total agreement between you and your underwater colleague regarding that plan.

Know Your Diving Spot

Before you dive, familiarize yourself with the location. Local divers can give you information on marine life, water depth, currents and visibility. This way you can avoid unwanted underwater surprises.

Never Dive Alone

A buddy can be a great photo assistant, carrying an extra camera, holding a flash or posing with the fish. More important, he can keep a watchful eye on water depth, diving time and air consumption. It's easy to lose track of such details when your mind is on getting that once-in-a-lifetime photograph. Your friend can also keep a lookout for poisonous coral and fish that can give you a bad sting or burn.

Don't Take Risks

Never endanger yourself or a buddy for the sake of a great picture. If you're running low on air, return to the boat, even if you see the fish you've been looking for for years. It's better to come back with a few unexposed frames in your camera than to be caught down below with no air.

from the camera and hold it off at arm's length. Looking through the viewfinder, you see the subject swimming back and forth and up and down. You shoot. What do you think the chances are that your flash was aimed at the fish?

Before you answer, think about refraction, which causes the subject to appear larger and closer than it actually is. If you think you might have aimed the flash slightly in front of the fish, or missed it completely, you are probably right.

Accurate aiming takes experience. You can practice framing a subject in the camera and aiming a separate flash at home. Chase your cat or dog around the living room and shoot a roll or two of flash pictures. When your photos come back from the lab, you'll see just how accurate your aim was.

After a few practice sessions like that on land, you can try it in the deceptive underwater environment. This is the important thing to remember: Things appear closer to you under water than they actually are. For example, if you're aiming your off-camera flash at a subject that looks three feet away, remember it's actually about four feet away. To compensate for this, aim the flash about a foot *behind* where you *see* the subject.

Get in the habit of always aiming the flash slightly behind where the subject seems to be. You can practice this technique in your local swimming pool.

CLOSE-UP PHOTOS

The best way to capture the minute detail of coral, fish and marine plants is with a macro lens. Because depth of field is always limited in close-up and macro work, you should use electronic flash. It enables you to use a small lens aperture.

Flash Position—The key to good illumination in your close-up shots is accurate flash placement. To avoid backscatter, use the flash off-camera. Try to aim the flash from a direction that doesn't cause shadows over important subject parts.

You can experiment with flash placement in shallow water anywhere. A quiet swimming pool is ideal. Even a filled-up bathtub will do. Place some rocks or shells in the water. Then photograph them with the flash aimed from different directions. Write down details of how each photo was lit, or make simple lighting sketches. Compare these with the processed photos.

Warning—Water and electricity can be a dangerous combination. You must *always* be safety conscious—whether you're in the waters of the Caribbean or at home in your tub. Use only flash units that have been approved for underwater use by *Underwriters' Laboratories (UL).* Flash units without this approval may give you a severe or dangerous shock. Make sure you follow the operating instructions for the unit *precisely.*

Coral reefs offer an abundance of colorful plant and coral life. In this environment, you can find many ideal subjects for close-up photography.

At a depth of 40 feet, these pink sweepers looked blue to us. By daylight, they would have recorded that way on film. We captured their true color by using electronic flash at a distance of three feet from the fish.

Photographing your diving buddies is fun. However, getting someone to remain in one place under water isn't always easy. If possible, have your subject hold onto something, such as part of a shipwreck or a piece of dead coral.

Exposure need not always be "accurate." The tube sponge in this photo was actually white. To record maximum detail and for dramatic impact, we underexposed. Bracket your exposures and select the one you like best at your leisure, when you're back home.

It's virtually impossible to catch a fish with your hands. However, it's fun trying—and having someone photograph the attempt.

Much of the underwater world is delicate and fragile. While you enjoy it, take care not to damage it. It is a priceless heritage for those following you.

This dramatic picture was made against the light and carefully timed for the moment both divers released air. Much of the impact of this photo would have been lost without the sparkling air bubbles. The two divers had just descended and were checking their equipment. In diving, *safety* always comes *first!*

PROTECT THE ENVIRONMENT

As scuba diving becomes more popular, the underwater environment becomes threatened. When you're diving, help to preserve the beauty and health of our coral reefs.

Did you know that coral is a living organism—an "animal" with its skeleton on the outside? Don't sit or stand on coral. It's fragile and breaks easily. Never break off a piece as a sample or souvenir.

Coral grows very slowly. Some species grow less than one inch per year. It is also susceptible to infection when its outer skeleton is damaged.

Read up on the delicate balance of the reef ecosystem. Educate others to preserve the environment. Only with the help and care of all divers will our underwater world be preserved for generations to come.

3 Shooting at the Beach

During an entire day at the beach, you shouldn't run out of picture-taking possibilities. At sunrise, for example, you can photograph fishermen casting for a tasty meal, sea gulls gliding on air currents and joggers out for their morning exercise. You can shoot with the sun behind you, to get photos full of detail. Or, you can shoot with the sun behind the subject, to make dramatic silhouettes.

Around midday, when the light is at its brightest, you can get great close-up shots of shells, crabs and rocks. Be creative with filters to produce a wide variety of effects.

The beautiful low lighting of late afternoon is ideal for portraiture and glamour photography. That is also good light for taking pictures of family, friends and fellow beachgoers having a great time. Photograph them in or out of the water.

Just before sunset, when the low sun causes dramatic shadows, you can capture interesting patterns and textures in the sand.

SALT, SAND, WATER AND WIND

Three elements at the beach can be harmful to your equipment. They are salt, sand and water. If these elements get on or in your camera or lens, they can also ruin your pictures. Another damaging factor is wind. It is the carrier of sand and salt spray. Protect your equipment especially well on windy days.

When used skillfully, props can play an important part in beach photography. Here, the beach umbrella occupies about half the picture area without detracting from the subject. Without this colorful prop, the same scene would be much less eye-catching. Photo by Lou Jones.

Sunrise and sunset are often the most spectacular times at the beach. To get your best beach pictures, get there early or be prepared to stay late. As this picture shows, it's well worth it. Photo by John Isaac.

As little as a single grain of sand can cause problems inside your camera. It can jam the film-advance lever, shutter-speed dial, focusing ring or aperture ring.

Ocean water is perhaps your camera's worst enemy. Its spray contains corrosive salt that will literally eat your camera. But moisture alone can jam your camera controls and short-circuit the electronics, as well as ruin film.

Salt spray on the front element of a lens can have a soft-focus effect on photographs. If it gets on the viewfinder eyepiece, the salt can make viewing and focusing difficult.

We've already discussed camera care and cleaning in Chapter 1. Be sure you've read it thoroughly before shooting at the beach.

PROTECTIVE COVERING

When we pack our camera bags for a day at the beach, we include the following protective gear:

Plastic Bags—Plastic sandwich bags are invaluable at the beach. You can place your camera in a bag and cut an opening for the lens. You'll be able to shoot freely while your camera is protected against the elements. We also put lenses and accessories we're not using into plastic bags. This gives them added protection in the camera bag from salt in the air and sand that may be kicked up accidentally.

Maximum Protection—A waterproof plastic-bag housing, specially designed for underwater photography, offers maximum protection for a camera. This is true not only for underwater use, but also by the seashore.

CLEANING KIT

The following inexpensive items will help keep your camera and lens clean at the beach. They can make the difference between great photos and no photos at all.

Soft, Clean Cloth—Salt spray builds up surprisingly fast on the front surfaces of lenses and filters. The closer you get to the water, and the windier it is, the more rapid the build-up. Have a soft, clean cloth handy to remove the spray.

Check the lens frequently. If there's a noticeable salt deposit, wipe it off *very gently.* If you rub too hard, you may scratch the lens surface or damage the lens

When a child is in "paradise," we don't like to intrude. To keep our distance, we use a long lens. This has an added advantage: It gives us spontaneous shots that are only possible when the subject is unaware of being photographed.

When waves are crashing or children are splashing near you, protect your camera well from the salty water. You can put the camera in a plastic sandwich bag and cut an opening for the lens. For better protection, use a commercially available plastic-bag housing.

coating. Rub in a circular motion, working from the center of the lens to its rim.

Lens Cleaner—Special lens-cleaning fluid, available at camera stores, is helpful in removing salt spray, dust, fingerprints and suntan lotion from a lens or filter. Apply the lens cleaner sparingly to the soft, clean cloth. Never put the fluid directly on a lens or filter.

Blower Brush—Always be on your guard against sand getting near your camera. If sand does settle on camera or lens, use a small blower brush to remove the grains. Pay special attention to the camera controls.

SUNRISE AND SUNSET

To get the most dramatic photos on the beach, be there early and stay late. Record the beauty of sunrise and sunset.

Film—You can use any color-slide or print film in the ISO 64/19° to ISO 200/24° speed range. If you use a film of ISO 400/27° or faster, you may get an overexposed image, even with the shortest exposure the camera is capable of giving.

Lens—The longer the lens focal length, the bigger the sun will be in the photo. If you want the sun to fill most of the frame, shoot with a 400mm, 500mm or 600mm lens. For a sunrise or sunset in which the sun is only one of many components in the scene, you can shoot with a lens of shorter focal length. Usually, it'll be a standard 50mm lens. If you want to include a wider-than-normal scene, use a wide-angle lens.

Exposure—At sunrise and sunset, the brightness of the light changes rapidly. As the sun rises above the horizon in the morning, the lens aperture/shutter-speed combination for correct exposure changes almost continuously.

We have found that the best way to deal with a rapid change in light conditions is to use the camera on automatic. If we're shooting with slide film, we take additional exposures at one and two *f*-stops under the recommended setting. These additional exposures assure us of saturated colors in the sky. If you overexpose the sky in your slides it will appear pale and washed-out.

When we photograph sunrise or sunset on negative film, we generally don't bracket exposures. Negative film has a relatively wide exposure range. Your exposure can be slightly inaccurate and you'll still get a good picture. However, with negative film slight overexposure is preferable to underexposure.

Modern processing labs can perform "magic" with negatives. They can lighten, darken or shift color balance, as requested. Just ask for the effect you want. But be prepared to pay a custom-job price.

Remember these basic rules: Expose slide film for the highlight areas. You'll get good color, except in the deepest shadows. You won't get any colorless, washed-out areas. Expose color and b&w negative film for the shadow areas. This will generally give you tonal detail throughout the image.

Tripod—When the sun is below the horizon, there is often a beautiful glow in the sky. To capture this dramatic natural-light display, you may need to shoot at a slow shutter speed. This will require the use of a tripod to hold the camera steady.

Time-Lapse Sequence—You can capture a sequence of shots of the setting sun. Start shooting when the sun is not quite touching the horizon. Shoot until the last red glow in the sky dies away. An intervalometer or automatic timer is useful for this. It automatically releases the shutter repeatedly at the time interval you have selected. We use a *Minolta Multi-Function Back.* It can be programmed to operate the camera at intervals ranging from one second to one hour. At sunset, we program the unit to take an exposure every 30 seconds.

This way, we expose a 36-frame roll of film in 18 minutes. From the 36 photos, we select the best 10 or 12 to make an interesting sequence.

Another useful accessory for photographing a sunrise or sunset is an automatic film-advance unit. A motor drive or auto winder lets

If you want to create a sunset effect in the middle of the day, use a sunset filter on the lens. However, avoid "giveaways" that would indicate the time of day, such as very short, hard shadows.

you concentrate on the scene without the worry of advancing the film.

Reflector Card—When shooting backlit portraits, a reflector card that can bounce light onto the subject is useful. The card can be mounted on a stand or tripod or can be held by an assistant. White reflector cards produce a soft light. Tinfoil reflectors give a harder, more dramatic, light effect.

Reflector cards can be made or bought in just about any size. You may need only a small, two-foot-square card to bounce just a little light. For a full-length portrait of two people, you may need a six-foot-square reflector card.

You can control the amount of light reflected by a card by changing the card-to-subject distance, and also its angle. The closer the card is to the subject, the more light will reflect onto the subject.

SILHOUETTES

At sunrise and sunset, you can get beautiful silhouettes of people at the beach. A silhouette is a dark image, outlined against a bright background.

To create a silhouette against a low sun, have the sun behind the subject. Expose for the sky, to get a colorful effect. The subject will record in silhouette.

When you are shooting silhouettes with slide film, avoid overexposure of the sky. A little underexposure is usually best. It gives more saturated colors in the sky. Don't underexpose print film, however, or you may lose tonal detail in the sky.

LIGHT METERING

Exposure metering doesn't always involve simply pointing your automatic camera and shooting. On a beach, where backgrounds are generally lighter than nearby subjects, special metering techniques are called for.

Close-Up Meter Reading—If you try to photograph a backlit subject with your camera set on automatic, you'll get a perfectly exposed picture—of the background. The subject will be underexposed. This condition is made worse when sunlight is reflected by sand or water. If you're deliberately shooting a silhouette, this is OK. But if you want detail in the subject, you have to take special care when metering.

To ensure a correctly exposed subject in backlighting, take a close-up meter reading. If your camera has an automatic-exposure (AE) lock, take a close-up reading of the subject's face. Lock the reading in, take your original position, and shoot. If your camera doesn't have an AE lock,

We took these photos at almost the same moment. Exposure was automatic in each case. The pictures illustrate well what a great difference lighting angle can make. For the top photo, the lighting was almost frontal. This recorded detail in the fisherman and highlighted the white surf. However, it provided no sparkle in the distant ocean. For the bottom photo, there was backlighting. It added sparkle to the water but put the fisherman in silhouette.

Both photos were made with an averaging meter in the camera, which was set for automatic exposure. For the left picture, the exposure indicated by the meter was given. The background is well-exposed but the backlit children are in silhouette. To make the right photo, we set the camera's exposure-compensation dial to +1-1/2. The additional exposure ensured some detail in the child. Notice that the ocean is less well defined in this picture. The cause of this is less depth of field, due to the larger lens aperture used.

take a close-up reading and remember the exposure setting. Manually set the *f*-stop and shutter speed and shoot from your chosen position.

Spot Meter—A spot meter allows you to take a reading of a small portion of your subject, even from a relatively long distance. We use one whenever we want to remain unobtrusive. You can meter an angle as small as 1° with a spot meter. This means you can meter the subject's face from a relatively long distance.

Incident-Light Meter—An incident-light meter measures the light falling on a subject, not the light reflected from it. To use the meter, hold it close to the subject and point its translucent light-gathering hemisphere at the light source. If you can't get close to the subject, position the meter so the light falling on it is about equal to the light falling on the subject.

Because the meter isn't pointed at the subject, it can't be misled by a bright background. It recommends an exposure that reproduces a typical subject well, regardless of the background.

Meter Your Hand—You may not own a spot meter or incident-light meter. Or, you may not have a chance to take a close-up reading. You have another alternative. All you need is your SLR's meter and your hand. Take a close-up reading of the palm of your hand. Your hand must be in the same lighting as the subject. For example, be sure that you're not in shadow when the subject is in direct sunlight.

With the camera set to the reading for your palm, you should get a photograph underexposed by about one step of a subject of average tonality. Therefore, for correct exposure, open the aperture one *f*-stop or increase exposure by one shutter-speed step.

CHILDREN AT PLAY

Children enjoy the natural playground of the beach. Here, they can forget about the trials and tribulations of growing up. They can concentrate on more important matters, like building sand castles, chasing waves, collecting sea shells and digging for sand crabs.

At these carefree times, children don't like to be bothered by photographers. Therefore, you should use a relatively long telephoto lens. We usually photograph children at the beach with a 200mm or 300mm lens or a Minolta 100-500mm zoom lens. Usually, the kids don't even know we're photographing them.

Handholding Long Lenses—Handholding long lenses is usually not a problem at the beach, even with relatively slow films like Kodachrome 64 or Kodacolor VR 100. On a sunny day, there's enough light to use a fast enough shutter speed to eliminate the effect of camera shake. With a 300mm lens in bright sunlight, you can expose at 1/500 second at *f*-5.6. However, at that aperture your focus must be right on target. Take your time and focus carefully.

There's a rule-of-thumb for handholding lenses: Never use a shutter speed slower than the reciprocal of the lens focal length. Thus, if you are shooting with a 500mm lens, don't use a shutter speed slower than 1/500 second. To be extra sure, use a 1/1000 second. As long as you follow this rule, you'll be able to use long lenses at the beach without a tripod.

Subject Cooperation—To get the best children photos, you sometimes need their cooperation. In such cases you're not limited to a long lens. You also have more creative control.

You can sit or stand in the water to get an eye-level view of your subject. With a 28mm or 35mm lens, you can capture a child playing in the surf from just a few feet away. If you have the child run toward you, rather than across

At the beach, children become so absorbed in their activities that they're not easily distracted. Step lightly and be alert—and you'll get charming candid shots like this.

This photo was made from relatively near the subject. However, she was so intent on her important mission that she was totally unaware of the presence of a camera.

These "builders" were rightfully proud of their construction. Because sand is of uniform color and texture, hard side lighting is essential. It brings out a structure's shape in detail.

The main subject is King Kong and his "creators." However, notice that we were careful to include a section of ocean in the background. Without this indication of the location, the picture would look much less impressive.

Being buried in the sand is one of the rituals of a day at the beach. Low sunlight is best because it accentuates sand contours and texture.

your line of view, image blur will be minimized. If you shoot at a shutter speed of 1/60 second, the waves will blur slightly. This adds a feeling of movement and life to the photo.

Building Sand Castles—Children of all ages enjoy building sand castles. To photograph the activity unobtrusively, use a 200mm or 300mm lens. However, you have more scope for creative composition if you come close and use a wide-angle lens. You can shoot with the castle behind the children or you can shoot over the castle toward the children. You can include the whole scene. If you want to record close-up detail, use a lens with a longer focal length or a macro lens.

GLAMOUR PHOTOGRAPHY

The beach is an excellent setting for glamour photography. First, find an attractive model. Then, explore the seashore for a suitable location.

Location and Background—Try to select an area that offers a relatively plain background. Sand dunes, surf or simply a stretch of beach are all ideal. So are jetties, rocks and piers.

Avoid other people in the background. They will be distracting if they have no relationship to your subject. For example, a husband and wife, wearing matching plaid bathing suits, will destroy the mood of a photo of a young model in a designer swimsuit. Their presence will also interfere with the effectiveness of the composition.

Get to the beach early or stay late. You'll have a better chance of finding a location without a lot of people. You and your model will find it more comfortable and easier to shoot without curious onlookers around you. Early morning and late afternoon also offer the most suitable lighting. The sun is low, so there are no deep, unflattering shadows.

When you're shooting nudes, privacy is especially important. Some beaches don't permit nude sunbathing; others welcome it. A *Guide to Nude Beaches,* published in 1982, lists the major beaches around the world permitting nudity. It's a useful source if you

For successful nude photography, there are two prerequisites: You need a secluded spot and warm weather. You and your model can work well only if you're reasonably sure to be free from intrusion and spectators. Warmth is essential if your model is to feel—and look—comfortable and relaxed. Photo by Lucien Clergue.

haven't yet found your own suitable location. Even when you're shooting at an officially recognized beach for nude sunbathing, find a private, secluded spot for your photography.

Makeup—The art of makeup at the beach involves *understatement.* Don't overdo it!

High-gloss lipstick helps to give a "wet and wild" look. A little rouge and some eye makeup can add color and contrast to the model's face. You can use suntan lotion to add luster to the model's body.

If you're not a makeup expert, don't worry. Most women are—by their late teens!

Posing the Model—You can't simply start shooting and expect great pictures. Even the most beautiful model in the world and the most idyllic setting don't automatically guarantee it. If you want professional-looking glamour photographs, you have to *direct* the model.

Keep Your Distance—Don't shoot from too close. If you do, you'll get a distorted, unflattering image. For head-and-shoulder shots, shoot from no less than six feet. For full-length photos, don't get closer than about 12 feet. Use a lens of appropriate focal length.

Experiment With Expressions—Don't always have your model looking at the camera with a big smile. Experiment with serious, sensual and pensive expressions. When you do want the model to smile, ask her to smile with her mouth open, showing her teeth. Then shoot several frames with a closed-mouth smile. In a full-length glamour or nude photo, you needn't always see the face.

Experiment with many poses and expressions and shoot a lot of film. When your processed photos come back from the lab, keep the best and learn from the worst.

Hands—In a glamour photograph, the position of the hands is important. They should be resting in a comfortable position or doing something natural and believable. You can ask the model to run her fingers through her hair, with her head tilted slightly back or to one side. This will convey a feeling of spontaneity. Avoid having the elbows pointing toward the camera. This foreshortens the arms in an unattractive way.

Hands should not distract the viewer of the photograph. For example, hands on hips with fingers spread apart may attract too much attention. It's better to have the hands closed, with the knuckles resting on the hips.

Hands can be used to frame the face gracefully. However, they should not cover important features. And, the pose should always look natural and comfortable.

Action—Glamour photographs don't always have to show the model standing, sitting or reclining. Many of today's top glamour photographers like to add *movement* to their photographs. With a motor drive or auto winder and a fast shutter speed, you can take spectacular studies of motion.

You can photograph a model in a bathing suit or sun suit running through shallow surf. During the early-morning and late-afternoon hours, backlighting accentuates the water particles kicked up by the model.

Encouragement—You have probably seen fashion-photography sessions on television. You've heard a photographer tell his model, "That's super. You look great. Hold that terrific pose. Wonderful." That's encouragement or positive reinforcement. Remember, you and your model are a team. The outcome of your efforts depends on both of you. Encourage her as you go along.

Props—Appropriate props can give your photos a theme. Props need not be elaborate to be effective. Pose a model standing in the water, holding a scuba mask in her right hand and swim fins in her left. She'll look like a modern, sports-minded woman.

Other effective props are colorful beach umbrellas and towels. Lifeguard platforms and boats also make interesting props. You can pose your model on them or use them as backgrounds. A slightly out-of-focus lifeguard in the background can add to the interest of a photo without distracting attention from the model.

Soft-Focus Attachment—Direct sunlight can be harsh. A soft-focus attachment on the camera lens diffuses and softens the image. It can add a dream-like quality to a photo. A soft-focus attachment also helps eliminate minor blemishes and wrinkles on the subject's skin.

Reflectors—Deep shadows, due to direct sunlight, are rarely flattering. Such shadows are softened somewhat by the bright surrounding sand and water on a beach. However, reflector cards give you control over the lighting. You can soften shadows to the extent you consider desirable.

You can purchase reflectors of various kinds from photo dealers. You can also make your own from white cardboard or cardboard covered with tin foil. Reflectors can be supported on tripods or light stands. Or, they can be held by a friend.

In the middle of the day, you can use a foil reflector to redirect the light from the overhead sun to hit the model from a lower angle. When the sun is low, you can use direct sunlight for backlighting and reflected sunlight from the front as main light.

Electronic Flash—Instead of using a reflector to brighten shadows or illuminate a backlit subject, you can use electronic flash. Use it to supplement the existing light. To retain some shadows, the flash exposure should be less than the existing-light exposure. Here's what you do to achieve this kind of *fill flash:*

Set the camera shutter to the flash sync speed—usually 1/60 second. Take an existing-light meter reading. Let's assume it's 1/60 second at *f*-11. Set the lens aperture to *f*-11. Use the flash guide number, supplied with your flash unit, to calculate the flash-

With a careful balance of flash and natural light, you can make spectacular beach photos. Exposure for the evening sky was calculated to achieve the dramatic background in this photo. Enough flash was added to record detail in the model. Photo by Robert Farber.

You needn't pack your camera away when the sky is overcast. Soft light is ideal for some subjects. Uniform illumination from sky and sand ensure a soft-looking image. Notice the brightness and detail in the face, in spite of the large brim of the hat. Photo by Robert Farber.

to-subject distance for an *f*-11 aperture. Do this by dividing the guide number by the *f*-stop. Let's say the guide number is 88 (feet). The recommended subject distance is then 88/11 feet or eight feet.

Because you want the flash only for *supplementary* light, you should move the flash slightly farther away from the subject. Bracket exposures by varying the flash-to-subject distance. In the above example, make exposures with the flash 10, 12 and 14 feet from the subject.

For more ideas for glamour photographs, see *How to Photograph Women* and *Pro Techniques of People Photography,* both published by HPBooks.

SURFERS AND WINDSURFERS

When the conditions are right, you may see surfers riding on the crests of waves. Or, you may encounter windsurfers being propelled at impressive speeds by the forces of mother nature. You can capture the action of these fast-paced sports.

Depending on where the waves are breaking, your subject may be anywhere from 25 yards to several hundred yards offshore. To fill the frame with the subject, you'll need a telephoto lens or a tele-zoom.

We generally use a 100-500mm zoom lens. The continuously variable focal lengths provided by this lens enable us to crop quickly and tightly in the viewfinder. We can work fast and accurately, regardless of constantly changing subject distance. We set the shutter to 1/500 second or faster.

A tripod or unipod is useful to steady the camera and telephoto lens. With its three legs, a tripod offers maximum support and stability. A unipod, with only one leg, requires a more conscious effort on your part to hold the camera steady. Tripod or unipod can make framing, focusing and holding the camera easier. When you are photographing a fast-moving subject with a heavy telephoto lens, this support makes following the action in the viewfinder easier.

Motor Drive or Auto Winder— Surfers and windsurfers can be riding high one second and completely submerged the next. Good timing makes the difference between a great photo of a surfer, sometimes in midair, and nothing but a big splash. To capture the exact moment you want, shoot with a motor drive or auto winder. By using a motor drive on the fastest frames-per-second (fps) speed, you have the best chance of getting the shot you want.

Film—On a bright day, you can use Kodachrome 64 and shoot at 1/500 second at *f*-5.6. This shutter speed is fast enough to stop the action. However, the relatively wide aperture requires you to focus very accurately. With ISO 400/27° film, you can shoot at 1/500 second with the aperture set between *f*-11 and *f*-16. This gives you more depth of field.

BIRDS IN FLIGHT

Sea gulls fly over the beaches constantly, looking for a snack. Capturing the graceful motion of birds in flight is not difficult if you know a few tricks.

Feeding—By offering a tasty treat, such as popcorn, bread or pretzels, we get birds to hover directly over our heads. When we toss the food in the air, the birds come flocking.

Exposure—We have found the best way to ensure correct exposure of a sea gull flying overhead is to shoot on automatic. Your in-camera meter will read mainly the sky. The sky will record an attractive midtone blue. The tone of the gull will depend on the position of the sun relative to gull and camera.

When you're shooting against an overcast sky, you can silhouette the gulls. Expose for the light sky. The gulls will record as dark forms, with little detail.

Making a deliberate composition of gulls in midair is virtually impossible. Shoot lots of pictures, using a motor drive, if you have one. When your films are processed, select the best pictures.

Lens—The number of birds hovering over you changes constantly. So does their distance from each other and their height.

This is a good example of thoughtful framing. The archway directs the viewer's attention into the scene. The arch serves another purpose: It gives the picture a feeling of depth or distance.

Sea gulls are always willing models as long as there's food about. Here, you can see three gulls heading for the same piece of popcorn.

For quick framing, nothing beats a zoom lens. Our 35-105mm zoom helps us get good shots of single birds and of groups.

Diving Birds—Birds don't just fly. Some of them dive. In the warm waters off the southern United States, you'll see pelicans diving at fast speeds on unsuspecting fish. They usually dive several times in one general location. You can focus on that area of the water while the bird is overhead. If you shoot with a zoom lens, you have a good chance of recording the decisive moment in an attractive composition.

Shutter Speed—To freeze the action of a bird in flight, you'll need to shoot with a fast shutter speed. Use 1/500 second or faster. For a photo that conveys a feeling of motion, you may want to experiment with slow shutter speeds. For example, 1/30 second exposure will blur the subject enough to suggest motion in the photo. To avoid unwanted camera movement at relatively long exposure times, use a tripod or unipod.

Shooting at the same slow shutter speed won't give you the same result twice. The birds will be flapping their wings at different rates and flying at different speeds.

FILTERS

Throughout a day of shooting at the beach, you'll encounter several shooting situations that might require the use of filters. They were mentioned briefly in the *Equipment* chapter. Here are more details about the main filters we find helpful.

SKYLIGHT FILTER

A skylight filter reduces the blue cast caused by ultraviolet (UV) radiation present in most beach scenes. Film is inherently sensitive to UV. The slight pink color of a skylight filter also helps keep flesh tones looking natural by removing excess blue.

A skylight filter is never harmful to the images you produce. It can be left on a camera lens permanently. This makes it ideal protection for the front element of the lens, keeping off sand, salt spray, fingerprints and suntan lotion. The filter is easy to remove and clean. If you scratch or otherwise damage a skylight filter, it is relatively inexpensive to replace. Replacement or repair of a lens would cost you a lot more.

POLARIZING FILTER

A polarizing filter is perhaps the most useful filter at the beach. It can enhance a scene in several ways. It can darken the blue sky, reduce reflections from water and glare from sand, and increase color saturation.

You can rotate the polarizing filter on the lens. You can see the effect of this on the image through the camera viewfinder.

Briefly, here's how a polarizing filter works: Normally, light waves vibrate in all directions perpendicular to the direction of the light ray. *Polarized* light waves vibrate in only *one* direction. A polarizing filter transmits *only* light waves vibrating in one direction. If the polarizer is oriented appropriately, it will exclude polarized light.

Following are some examples of polarized light being controlled by a polarizing filter to achieve a photographic effect:

Darken Blue Sky—When the sun and the blue sky subtend an angle of 90° at the camera position, the light from the sky is polarized. This polarized light can be eliminated or reduced, depending on the rotational orientation of the polarizer. By darkening the blue sky in this way, you increase cloud-to-sky contrast. You do this without affecting the overall color balance of a photo.

Here's a simple method of finding the part of the blue sky where the light is polarized. Hold your hand so your thumb and index finger form a right angle. Point your thumb at the sun. The skylight has maximum polarization anywhere your index finger can now point.

Eliminate Reflections—Non-polarized light becomes polarized when it is reflected from nonmetallic surfaces, including water, at a certain angle. When the angle between the reflecting surface and the light beam is about 32° to 35°, the reflected light is fully polarized. With a polarizing filter, you can eliminate or reduce that reflected light.

You don't always want to eliminate reflection completely. Sparkling reflections on water can look very dramatic. If you take away *all* the sparkle, your photo may look dull and drab. By rotating the polarizing filter, you can control the amount of reflection removed. If you want to see objects under water, you'll want to eliminate surface reflections completely.

Increase Color Saturation—The 32° to 35° angle of reflection that produces polarized light doesn't apply only to water. A reflection from a beach umbrella, brightly painted lifeboat or beach house at that angle is also polarized light. That polarized surface reflection can be eliminated with a polarizing filter. The colors of the surface are recorded with more brilliance when the surface reflection has been removed.

If a sunset isn't colorful enough, left, you can still take home a dramatic photograph, right, by using a red, orange or sunset filter on the camera lens.

COLOR-CONTROL FILTERS

When shooting with daylight-balanced film, you shouldn't need color filters at the beach. However, in a few situations the daylight may be affected in such a way that it doesn't accurately match the built-in color balance of the film. To help control color, the following three filter types are available:

Color-Compensating (CC) Filters—These filters enable you to control one color at a time. They are available in cyan, magenta, yellow, red, green and blue. Each color comes in a range of strengths, from 05 to 50.

If you're shooting a subject under bright green foliage, the subject will take on a green color imbalance. You can lessen or remove this imbalance with the use of a magenta CC filter of appropriate strength. A CC10M or CC20M will probably do the job.

Or, suppose you're taking a portrait of a woman in a wide-rimmed yellow hat. The rim will cause a yellow color cast on her face. You can eliminate this with the use of a blue CC filter.

Light-Balancing Filters—Instead of changing only one color, as do CC filters, light balancing filters change the spectral character of the light. They change the *color temperature* of the illumination.

Wratten filters in the 82 series are bluish. They make the illumination more blue. Wratten filters in the 81 series are amber. They make the illumination more reddish.

Color-Conversion Filters—These filters are similar to light-balancing filters, but stronger. They correct for a greater color imbalance in the illumination.

Wratten filters in the 80 series are blue and remove a reddish imbalance. Filters in the 85 series are amber and remove a blue imbalance.

Typical Application—Here are a few situations where you may want to control the color balance of a scene or subject.

On an overcast day, when the light is distinctly bluish, use an amber filter in the 81 series. These filters *warm* the illumination, making it more reddish.

If the sky is blue and your subject is in the shade, the sky will give the subject a bluish cast. To correct for this imbalance, you can use the strongest 81-series filter. If the color imbalance is great, you may need a filter in the stronger 85 color-conversion series.

If you are shooting a portrait on a clear day at sunset with your subject facing the sun, his face will look reddish. An 82-series filter helps reduce this imbalance. If the strongest filter in the 82 series is not strong enough, use a blue filter in the 80 series.

FILTERS FOR B&W FILM

Red, yellow and orange filters can be used to darken blue sky and increase contrast between clouds and sky when you're shooting on b&w film. A red filter will give a dramatic dark sky. A yellow filter will darken the blue sky only slightly. An orange filter will give an inbetween effect.

Here's a simple rule for general contrast control in b&w photography: A filter makes its own color brighter in a print. It makes other colors darker. For example, imagine a girl in a red bathing suit, against a blue sky. A blue filter will make her swimsuit nearly black and lighten the sky. A red filter will make the suit appear very light and the sky very dark.

NEUTRAL-DENSITY (ND) FILTERS

Neutral-density filters reduce the amount of light entering the lens without affecting color. The filters are identified in one of two ways. They may be marked ND1, ND2 and ND3. These filters reduce the light by one, two and three exposure steps respectively. Some filters have density values engraved on the filter ring. The accompanying table shows what the density values mean.

Neutral-density filters can be useful on the beach. For example, you may take ISO 1000/31° film to capture pre-dawn and dusk scenes. These filters enable you to use the same film during the bright midday-sunlight hours.

ND filters are useful for controlling *f*-stops and shutter speeds in brightly-lit situations. For example, say you want to blur the graceful motion of sea gulls flying overhead. If you have ISO 1000/31° film in your camera, you may not be able to shoot at a shutter speed as slow as 1/30 second to blur the action. An ND filter enables you to lengthen the exposure to create the desired effect.

You can also use ND filters to give you a larger working aperture. For example, say you are shooting a portrait and you want an aperture of *f*-2.8 for an unsharp background. With fast film, you may not be able to use a shutter speed to match that *f*-stop for correct exposure. The solution is to use a neutral-density filter to reduce the amount of light entering the lens.

A through-the-lens (TTL) exposure meter compensates for any filter on the camera lens. It indicates correct exposure with the ND filter in place.

Neutral density filters are also used for exposure control in mirror lenses, which have no adjustable aperture.

CREATIVE FILTERS

The name *creative filter* applies to a wide range of filters and light modifiers that can enhance an

EFFECT OF NEUTRAL-DENSITY FILTERS

Filter Density	Exposure Reduction (exposure steps)
0.1	1/3
0.2	2/3
0.3	1
0.4	1-1/3
0.5	1-2/3
0.6	2
0.7	2-1/3
0.8	2-2/3
0.9	3
1.0	3-1/3

The photographer wanted to blur the sand falling from the girl's hand. The camera was loaded with fast film. It would not permit a slow enough shutter speed, even at the smallest lens aperture. To make possible the use of a slow shutter speed, a neutral-density filter was used on the camera lens. Photo by Lucien Clergue.

image. If you think a blue sky would look better orange, you can use a *sunset filter.* If you think a rainbow would look good in a scene, you can add one with a *rainbow filter.* If you want to change a scene in a dozen different ways, you can do so.

Graduated Filters—These filters are half clear and half colored. They come in a variety of colors, including light blue, dark blue, orange, pink, green and red. They are called *graduated filters* because the color density builds up gradually from the middle of the filter toward the edge. These filters permit you to add color to only a portion of a scene—top, bottom, left or right.

A deep-blue graduated filter can add blue to gray sky without affecting the color of the sand on the beach. Mounted upside down, the filter can intensify the blue of the water without affecting the sky.

A graduated red filter is great for adding emphasis to a sunset or sunrise. A graduated orange filter can give a midday scene the appearance of sunset.

Fog and Mist Filters—These filters can give a sunlit scene a misty appearance. They diffuse the light entering the lens and reduce harsh shadows. The filters are available in several diffusion grades, from light mist to heavy fog.

Star Filter—This is a clear glass with a cross-line pattern. The pattern causes intense points of light to record as stars. Star filters can convert points of reflected light on water into beautiful starbursts.

You can choose a filter that will give stars with two, four, six, eight or 16 points. We find the 16-point star a little too confusing in most pictures. The two-point star we find a little too dull. For the best effect, the background to the stars should be dark.

You can easily make your own star filter with a piece of fine wire screen or nylon stocking. Place the screen or stocking material over the lens as you would a filter.

Rainbow Filter—It consists of clear glass with a transparent rainbow painted on it. It can turn a scene with a dull, colorless sky into a dramatic photograph.

The possibilities with creative filters are endless. Filter manufacturers' manuals outline some of the effects that can be achieved. These booklets are available at camera stores or from filter manufacturers or distributors.

ABSTRACT IMAGES

The beach offers many opportunities for shooting abstract images created by sand, surf, wind, light and shade. Seeing these themes is one thing; capturing them on film is another. You'll get the most interesting abstract images in the early morning and late afternoon. At those times, the sun's low position in the sky creates dramatic shadows and patterns.

Train your eye to focus selectively on a small portion of a scene, eliminating the surrounding area.

CLOSE-UPS

The beach is a natural studio for close-ups. Subjects, lighting and props are all there, ready for your use. Colorful sea shells, crabs and water-worn rocks all make interesting subjects for close-up photography. When these subjects are photographed on a sunny day against a background of sand, detail and color come alive.

Macro Lens—The easiest way to get close-ups at the beach is with a macro lens. Most 50mm macro lenses feature a minimum focusing distance of less than one foot. Macro lenses of 100mm focal length have a slightly longer minimum focusing distance.

If you want to get close enough to the subject for a 1:1 (life-size) reproduction, you can use a 1:1 adapter in conjunction with a macro lens. These adapters are often included when you buy a macro lens. They can also be purchased separately.

We use both the 50mm and the 100mm macro lens. They do double duty as standard lens and

The ingredients making up this simple scene were sand, wind, light and shade. However, it required an alert photographer to translate the subject into an attractive photograph. Photo by Lucien Clergue.

medium telephoto lens respectively. This helps to keep our camera bag light—an important consideration on a long day at the hot beach.

Small Aperture—In close-up photography, depth of field is always limited. The smaller the *f*-stop, the more you will have in focus. If you want only a specific feature of a subject in focus, such as the eyes of a crab, shoot at a wider aperture. But be sure to focus accurately.

With a 35mm SLR, you view the scene at the widest lens aperture. The lens automatically closes down to the picture-taking aperture at the moment of exposure. There are ways to check depth of field, however. If the camera has a depth-of-field preview button, press it and the lens will stop down to the picture-taking aperture. This is the easiest and surest way of determining depth of field. However, you can also see how much of the subject will be in focus by checking the depth-of-field scale on the aperture ring of the lens.

Steady Grip—With a film in the ISO 64/19° to ISO 100/21° speed range, a small *f*-stop may require a relatively slow shutter speed, even on a bright day. Image blur is emphasized at close shooting distances because image detail is recorded larger. Hold the camera very steady. If you're shooting close-ups on the sand, wedge your elbows into the sand, breathe in and hold your breath while you make the exposure.

Mini Tripod—You can get a tiny tripod with short legs, made specifically for close-up photography. With your camera mounted securely on one of these, you can make exposures up to several seconds, unless it's very windy on the beach.

Most mini tripods have built-in ball-joint heads. They allow you to position the camera exactly the way you want it.

Small Reflectors—We've discussed the usefulness of reflectors on the beach earlier. When you're shooting close-ups, reflectors are just as useful. However, you need small ones that won't get in the way. White index cards make excellent reflectors for this purpose. Use them to reflect the sunlight into the shadows on the subject.

CAMPFIRE

After a day of shooting at the beach, there's nothing like relaxing around a campfire. Some beach authorities permit them; others don't.

Daylight-balanced color film will reproduce the attractive orange glow of the fire the way you see it. It reproduces the atmosphere of the scene best. However, if you want *accurate* color balance in your friends' faces, use a tungsten-balanced film. It is balanced approximately for the light from the fire. It will make skin tones appear natural but will destroy much of the warm atmosphere of the scene.

Use a fast film. Rate it at twice its speed if necessary. Then, have the lab push-process it to compensate for underexposure.

Exposure—With film rated at ISO 320/26°, try a starting exposure of about 1/30 second at *f*-2.8 or *f*-4. You may have to pose your subjects and ask them to remain still to avoid image blur at the slow shutter speed.

Rate the film at twice its speed, if necessary. Then, have the lab push-process it to compensate for underexposure.

The light from a campfire is not constant. The flames rise and fall and flicker. Take an exposure-meter reading of the faces around the fire. Then, bracket your exposures generously.

If you plan to record sea shells and other small detail on a beach, take a macro lens. A mini-tripod is also helpful. It enables you to secure your camera firmly near ground level.

4 Water Shows

Trained animals are a joy to watch and photograph. At water shows, you'll see dolphins leaping high out of the water to take fish from a trainer's mouth. Some dolphins and whales permit themselves to be used as water skis, giving their trainer a smooth ride around the pool.

You may see a trainer put his head in the mouth of a huge killer whale. A less spectacular feat, but also impressive, is man and sea lion juggling balls.

Many marine parks offer interesting side shows. You may see a keeper wading in shallow water among the sharks while hand-feeding them. There are pools where children can pet dolphins, and tanks with spectacular displays of tropical fish.

In this chapter, we'll tell you how to capture the excitement and action of water shows. We'll also give you some advice on how to take pictures of creatures in an aquarium.

BEFORE YOU LEAVE HOME

The following preparatory steps will help make your visit productive and rewarding:

Send for Brochures—Most marine parks offer colorful brochures that describe and depict the daily events. They often show the stages, pools and props for the various shows. There are usually pictures of some of the performers and sections of the audience. These information sheets can help you prepare your equipment and shooting strategy.

Prepare Equipment—Assemble the cameras, lenses, films and accessories you think will be most suitable. We've photographed at indoor and outdoor water shows in Florida, California and Massachusetts. One of our most useful lenses has been a 75-200mm zoom lens. The film we use most is ISO 200/24° color-slide film. With this combination, we're equipped to capture most of the action.

If you're going to shoot indoor water shows, you'll need flash. To photograph through aquarium windows, you'll find a wide-angle lens ideal.

Another tool that's been invaluable to us is a spot meter that reads a 1° angle of view. For example, when a dark brown sea lion is on a large, white stage, an exposure reading from an in-camera meter would cause underexposure of the sea lion. With the spot meter, we can be confident that we have an accurate reading of the sea lion.

Check the Weather—We always listen to the weather forecast to check whether we're going to get sunshine, clouds, rain or wind. Of course, we prefer a sunny day. But if the weather is going to be less than perfect, being forewarned at least gives us the opportunity to be equipped properly.

Dress Appropriately—If you plan to shoot close to where the action—and the water—is, be prepared to get wet. Wear shorts, a T-shirt and sandals. They are comfortable and dry quickly in the sun if they should get wet.

When we spend an entire day under the bright sun, we both wear sun visors. A visor serves a double purpose: It shades and protects the face and also helps keep direct sunlight from the camera viewfinder.

Here, peak action was recorded. Both the dolphin and the ball had reached approximately the top of their motion. They were momentarily still before they started to descend. Typically, the peak of the action also gives the most dynamic and meaningful picture.

Try to include the crowd in some of your pictures. A background like this helps to tell the story of your visit to the marine park. Happy faces, colorful clothing and lots of noise and movement make up much of the atmosphere that surrounded you there.

Rick was as close to these two "performers" as he could get. However, with a 75-200mm zoom lens he was able to frame the scene just as he wanted it. The 100mm setting gave this ideal composition.

SHOOTING LOCATION

Our first concern at a water show is finding the best shooting location. Consider the following factors before you select a seat:

Splash Zone—Take a good look around before you sit down. Avoid the "splash zone," usually marked with a warning sign—and a big puddle from the previous show! In that location, you and your equipment will get soaked when a killer whale hits the water after a high jump. If you really want to shoot from that area to get a specific shot, make sure your camera, lenses and accessories are well protected in plastic bags.

Mobility—You'll get the best and most varied photos if you can move about during the show. Attendants generally insist that you remain seated during a performance. Your best chance of *some* mobility during a show is in an aisle seat. However, always be considerate of the other people watching the show.

If there is a glass or plastic partition between the audience and the pool, go up high enough to enable you to shoot over the partition. Remember, it will get splashed and this will cause pictures shot through it to be blurry.

Time of Day—The time of day affects the position of the sun and, therefore, the lighting on a show's stage or pool. Water-show facilities usually post a schedule of daily events. Check this information, then plan your shooting day for optimum illumination at each show location.

For ideal lighting, have the sun behind you or at the side, at a moderately low angle. If possible, avoid overhead midday sunlight. Also avoid light from behind the subject unless you want a silhouette or other special effect.

Background—Try to get an undistracting background for your pictures. Usually, there will be a colorful stage, complete with the marine park's name in big, bold letters. If you sit directly opposite the stage, this will form a suitable background for the performers.

When you shoot dolphins jumping high in the air, however, you may get an unattractive background. You can often minimize the "clutter" by shooting from high in the stands. Unfortunately, from that position the leap will not appear as high and spectacular as from a lower viewpoint.

You can reduce the background area and blur what background there is by shooting with a telephoto lens at a wide aperture.

Spectators—If you sit to the left or right of the stage, you can often use the crowd as background for the performers. Use a wide-angle lens. To get the "performers" and nearby members of the crowd in sharp focus, shoot at a small lens aperture.

CAPTURING ACTION

The action at water shows is fast. This can make getting good,

This is another good example of peak action. Notice also how the frontal sunlight has highlighted the dolphin and the hoop to separate them from the trees in the background. For a small bonus, this picture has a touch of humor: Notice the bird sharing the stage with the performers.

sharp pictures difficult. Following are some techniques that will help you capture the action:

Prefocus—The action may be fast, but it is usually also predictable. For example, when a dolphin is going to jump high to take a fish out of a trainer's mouth, the trainer usually tells the spectators what's about to happen. This enables you to prefocus your camera on the trainer's face. Don't wait for the dolphin to leave the water before you focus, or you'll certainly miss the shot.

You can use the prefocus technique when you're told that a dolphin is going to jump through a hoop or a sea lion is going to catch a ball on his nose. Make sure you have enough depth of field to allow for slight variations in the subject's movements.

Peak of Action—When a performing animal leaps vertically into the air, it stops momentarily at its peak position before coming down again. At that moment, you can usually "freeze" the action at the relatively slow shutter speed of 1/125 second. The point of peak action also generally gives the most interesting and well composed picture.

Unless you're shooting rapid sequence photos with a motor drive, you'll have to be alert and anticipate the peak of the action.

Auto-Focus—One of the latest camera innovations is automatic-focus 35mm SLRs. Because these cameras do the focusing for you, they enable you to concentrate on the subject and on capturing the right moment on film.

An auto-focus camera can be very helpful at a water show. For example, a trick that is very popular consists of dolphins "walking" backward across the pool on their tails. With an auto-focus camera, you simply frame the subject and shoot.

If you want to shoot a series of pictures of this event with a regular camera, you have to rely on adequate depth of field to get each shot in the series sharp. You may not have time to refocus between shots.

Barriers, such as glass partitions or fences, can "fool" a sonar- or infrared-operated automatic focusing device. The camera will focus on the barrier instead of the more distant subject. The result is an unsharp image. Be sure the space between you and the subject is unobstructed.

PANNING

If you shoot at a fast shutter speed—1/500 or 1/1000 second—you'll be able to freeze a fast-moving subject on film. For a different effect, you can use the technique called *panning*. It adds a sense of motion to a picture by blurring the background without affecting subject sharpness. You can use this technique when dolphins or whales are jumping through hoops or over props in the water.

Some marine facilities present shows with human performers. Water-skiing routines can be exciting and present good opportunities for photography. The action is fast, so be alert for the right moment to shoot. To frame an image as perfectly as this, a zoom lens is invaluable.

For a successful pan, select a shutter speed of about 1/30 second. As the subject leaves the water, follow its movement in the viewfinder. When the subject is where you want to photograph it, release the shutter. To ensure a smooth pan, continue to follow the action with your camera for a second or so after you've made the exposure.

Keeping a moving subject in the same position in the viewfinder takes practice. To be sure of one good picture, photograph the same action several times.

SPLASHES AND SPRAY

Splashes and spray can add interesting highlights to pictures of performing water creatures. You'll see spectacular splashes when a dolphin or whale jumps out of the water and lands back in it. Often you'll see a trail of flying water behind a fast-moving animal.

We find that splashes and spray enhance water-show pictures by accentuating the action. When water particles are backlit, they are bright and prominent in a picture. When they are lit frontally, they are less visible.

BE ALERT

At a water show, there's a lot going on in a short time. A dolphin may jump out of the water at the right side of the pool. Moments later, another dolphin may be seen playing basketball with a trainer on the stage. This may be followed by another dolphin doing a flip in the center of the pool.

Stay alert for a good picture. When you see one, shoot—but fast. And try to anticipate what's coming next.

PEOPLE PICTURES

We like to concentrate some of our attention on photographing people in the stands. A child's reaction to a killer whale jumping out of the water with a trainer riding on his back is precious. Also, the collective reaction of a crowd to an unexpected feat can make for an interesting picture.

Most marine parks feature curved arenas. This curvature allows you to photograph people at the opposite end of the pool. To single out one person, you'll need a long telephoto lens in the 200mm to 300mm range. For a crowd reaction shot, you can use a standard or wide-angle lens. If you have an aisle seat, you have the greatest mobility. This gives you more freedom in selecting your subjects and composing your pictures as you want them.

Feeding and Petting Areas— Feeding and petting areas are popular locations at marine parks. Children love to hand-feed and pet dolphins—and you'll love recording the event on film.

You may see a good picture across the pool, or right next to you. For fast and accurate framing, a zoom lens is ideal.

Most underwater creatures move quickly. A sudden jump can cause an unexpected splash that can soak the crowd on the side of the petting pool. Also, after a huge animal hits the water, a wave can wash over the side of the pool. Be alert, so you can get a picture of the action. But be equally alert to protect your camera and equipment from getting soaked.

SHOOTING THROUGH GLASS

The huge open-air tanks at marine parks often have viewing windows through which you can see the scene under water. To get natural-looking underwater photos, follow these guidelines:

Fast Film—To record the relatively dark underwater scene and stop subject movement, use fast film. We recommend a film with a speed of ISO 400/27°. If you find that you must use a shutter speed slower than 1/125 second, shoot at those moments when your subject is relatively motionless.

Bracket Exposures—To ensure good pictures, bracket exposures. Estimating or metering underwater exposures is difficult. Bracket at least one exposure step in both directions.

Wide-Angle Lens—Remember that things appear closer—and larger—through water than through air. A wide-angle lens at *f*-8 or *f*-11 gives a wide field of view and good depth of field. We generally use a 24mm or 28mm lens. We simply wait until the dolphin, shark or turtle swims into the frame and shoot.

Use Red CC Filter—Underwater scenes have an inherent blue-green color cast. If you want to reduce this, try using a red Color Compensating (CC) filter. A CC20R filter should help. Don't be tempted to use too strong a filter. This would reduce the already low light level reaching the film to a point where exposures would be impractically long—even with fast film.

Lens Hood—With a lens hood on the camera, you can place the camera in direct contact with the glass. The hood shields the lens from unwanted reflections in the glass of signs, people and windows.

Don't Shoot Upward—Don't point the camera up toward the bright sunlight. If you do, the camera's meter will read this light and underexpose the subject. Shoot horizontally or downward, unless you are prepared to estimate the exposure or want to record a silhouette.

Don't Use Flash—Flash can cause problems when you shoot through glass on a tank. Don't use it. If you're standing away from the window and fire a flash, the flash will bounce right back to the camera lens and spoil your picture. The flash will also illuminate particles and air bubbles in the water, creating lots of white spots in your photo.

The sun illuminated the subject from behind. For a silhouette like this to be effective, the subject must have a clearly recognizable outline. When you view this photograph, you immediately know that a dolphin is being fed a fish. The blue sky forms an uncluttered background.

INDOOR WATER SHOWS

Some water shows are indoors. Use the same basic techniques we've discussed for outdoor shows. However, most indoor shows don't have sufficient illumination for existing-light photography. You'll need electronic flash. Here are some tips for getting great shots with flash:

Get Close—Sit as close as possible to the stage and the action to get maximum use of the light output from your flash.

Use Fast Film—We recommend a film with a speed of ISO 400/27°. The faster the film, the greater will be the maximum shooting distance of the flash. Alternatively, from a specific location a faster film allows you to use a smaller lens aperture for greater depth of field.

Check Flash Range—Each flash unit has a guide number. Before you go to a show, use the guide number to make sure your flash can be used at a distance of at least 20 feet with the film you plan to use.

Fast Recycling—You may want to use a motor drive for fast picture sequences. For your flash to recycle as fast as the motor drive advances the film, you'll need a power charger or power grip.

Take Lots of Pictures—An automatic flash can be "fooled" for various reasons. For example, reflections from splashing water may cause the flash to underexpose the subject. If you're using manual flash, the size of the arena will probably reduce the effective guide number of the flash, leading to possible underexposure. To ensure correctly exposed photos, expose many frames while bracketing by changing the lens aperture.

Some indoor water shows using light-sensitive electronics may prohibit flash pictures. Be considerate of your fellow spectators and obey any such ban.

AQUARIUMS

Many marine parks feature aquariums filled with colorful tropical fish. These tanks usually contain coral and sea plants, giving the appearance of a natural environment.

Aquariums generally have dim lighting. To get sharp images of fast-moving fish, you need to shoot at a relatively fast shutter speed—probably 1/125 second or 1/250 second. To use such shutter speeds, you'll need fast film. You'll also need to use a large lens aperture. This means shallow depth of field and the need for accurate focusing.

We usually photograph aquariums with a 20mm or 24mm lens. These lenses are fast, give a wide field of view and offer extensive depth of field.

For an unusual shot that shows both the underwater and above-water scene, frame your picture with the water line exactly in the middle of the frame. This technique is especially effective for photographing floating creatures that are only half submerged, such as turtles and frogs.

If you photograph an aquarium with flash, aim the flash toward the glass at an angle that does not allow the flash to reflect back to the lens.

PRACTICE MAKES PERFECT

Most marine parks present each show several times a day. If you think you missed a good shot the first time, go back a second and third time. Having seen the show once, you'll be able to anticipate the action. You won't be surprised when a dolphin suddenly does a triple flip in midair or when a sea lion kisses the trainer.

We often take our best shots at the second or third visit to a specific show.

To capture real interaction between sea creatures and members of your family, go to the petting and feeding pools. Photo courtesy of Sea World, San Diego.

A show isn't a show without interaction between performers and audience. As the trainer greets her dolphin friend, record the response of the crowd. Show general views and detailed close-ups.

To shoot the sequence shown below, we used a motor drive. If you don't have a motor drive, you can easily *create* a similar sequence, but it needs patience. Watch the act several times and shoot a different stage of it each time.

5 Scenic Views

You can shoot scenic views at lakes, rivers, ponds, streams, waterfalls and along the ocean shoreline. On a sunny day, colors will be rich and saturated. The scene will have good contrast and detail. If you want your pictures to look like impressionistic paintings, you can shoot through light fog or even rain. You can also "cheat" a little by using a fog or mist filter.

We live by a fairly large pond, have several streams and waterfalls nearby, and are only minutes away from the Hudson River. The shoreline and boat yards of this majestic river are fantastic. We've taken many pictures within a few miles of our home. It's fun documenting the neighborhood. You can do the same.

We have taken pictures during the early morning and late afternoon hours. We've spent beautiful days in the sunshine and less comfortable hours in the rain—all to get good photographs. We hope this chapter will help you take great views of water scenery.

When photographing scenic views, it is generally best to get everything in sharp focus. With a wide-angle lens, you'll usually have no problem achieving this. Depth of field is adequate for most scenes, even at a wide lens aperture. With a standard lens, you may need to stop the lens down to a small aperture if the closest element of the scene is only a few feet away, as in this picture. However, don't be afraid to put the foreground out of focus if it will achieve the pictorial effect you want.

LAKES AND PONDS

Pay special attention to three important elements when photographing large or small bodies of water. They involve working with reflections, recording distance and creating effective composition. Let's take a look at these elements individually.

REFLECTIONS

A scene is usually about two exposure steps brighter than its reflected image. Base exposure on the scene, unless the reflection is to be the main part of your photograph.

When the water is calm, you can have fun creating interesting photographs with mirror reflections. Try photographing people and their reflections. Have your model wear a flowing dress or a swim suit. The lighter the garment, the brighter the reflection. If you are in a secluded location, consider trying nude photography.

Include enough water foreground to ensure that the entire reflection will be in the picture. You can also have the model standing in the water. However, remember that only the part above water will be reflected.

You can have your model toss a stone in the water. This will momentarily disturb the mirror surface.

When there is some wind, the

water will be rippled and will not give a mirror reflection. However, other attractive reflections are created. When you shoot against the light, you'll record many bright catchlights. You can use a *star filter*, designed to convert each of the catchlights into a star.

When photographing a boat, or a building near the water's edge, try to include the reflection. Try to include it all. Don't cut off the mast of a boat or the top story of a building when framing the scene.

You can diffuse a mirror reflection by using a *graduated fog filter*. It diffuses half the image while not affecting the other half. This creates the effect of fog on the water but does not alter the above-water scene.

Beware of using graduated color filters when photographing reflections. For example, a graduated blue filter adds color to a gray sky, but the reflected image of the sky remains unchanged. This gives the photo an unnatural look.

DISTANCE

When you see a scene, you do so in three dimensions: height, width and depth. A photograph is two-dimensional. It has no depth. To create a realistic-looking image of a scene, you must simulate the feeling of distance.

Try to compose a scene with an object or person in the foreground. This creates an effective reference point to add a sense of scale to a photograph. It enables the viewer to better determine the size of the water body. Without such a foreground, water scenes often look flat and mundane.

A photograph is much more interesting if it includes a rowboat, an overhanging tree, reeds or a rock in the foreground. Or, have a person wade out a few yards in the water. Take the picture with your friend looking toward the horizon.

To include very close foreground detail, use a wide-angle lens. Use a small enough lens aperture to record the entire scene sharply.

COMPOSITION

When photographing bodies of water, the position of the horizon line plays an important part in effective image composition. In composing scenic views, try to avoid placing the horizon line in the middle of the picture. Cutting the scene in half usually makes for an uninteresting photograph.

Foreground detail adds interest and dimension to a scene. However, the foreground element must be placed carefully not to hide important distant detail. Notice how the anchor half frames the lighthouse without obstructing it.

High Horizon—When you want to emphasize the foreground, place the horizon line near the top of the frame. For example, you can use this technique at a pond covered with white lily pads, or if there are swimmers or small boats nearby.

Low Horizon—The blue sky may be filled with beautiful, white, puffy clouds or the sky may be bursting with color at sunrise or sunset. In such a case, the sky may be a more important part of the scene than the lake or pond. Place the horizon line low in the frame, giving emphasis to the sky.

Rule of Thirds—When you look through the viewfinder of your SLR camera, imagine that the frame is divided into vertical and horizontal thirds. These lines intersect at four points in the frame. Generally, a composition has most viewer impact when the main part of interest in the scene is placed near one of these key picture locations.

For example, imagine you're photographing a pond with a beautiful weeping willow tree by the waterline. You could compose the picture with the tree directly in the middle of the scene. However, you would get a more impressive, balanced composition by placing the tree in the right or left third of the picture.

WATERFALLS

We have photographed large waterfalls, such as Niagara Falls, and small waterfalls, such as the one at the end of our road.

How the moving water is recorded strongly influences the effect the picture conveys. You can create two different moods by either "freezing" or blurring the rushing water. We have also learned the pictorial value the mist in a waterfall can have.

WATER MOTION

When we photograph a waterfall, no matter what the size, we always select the shutter-speed setting carefully. We deliberately determine whether to blur or freeze the water.

A shutter speed of 1/500 second or faster will freeze the rushing water, creating a scene that is not normally seen. The apparently static water almost has the appearance of a solid object, frozen in space.

An exposure of 1/30 or 1/15 second will streak the falling water, to give it motion and create a lively and natural-looking photograph.

The streaking effect changes

The famous *Maid of the Mist* braves the spray below Niagara Falls. The spray is permanent, but the rainbow isn't. It is dependent on the position of the sun and you. The sun must shine on the spray frontally. As you can see, it's worth waiting for the right moment.

with the length of exposure time, the distance and size of the fall and the power, or speed, of the rushing water.

Experiment—Because you can't see how the moving water will look when photographed, it's a good idea to experiment with several shutter speeds, from 1/30 second to one or two seconds. Choose the best photos after processing. For future reference, make a note of the exposure times and the different effects they produce.

If you plan to use shutter speeds of 1/30 or 1/15 second, use slow film, such as Kodachrome 25. With a medium-speed film, you may need a neutral-density filter on the camera lens to reduce the light to a level that will enable you to use a slow enough shutter speed.

Tripod—With shutter speeds of 1/60 second or slower, shoot with the camera on a tripod. Otherwise, not only will the water be blurred, but the remainder of the scene also.

RAINBOW

The mist around large waterfalls usually generates a rainbow. The key to seeing a rainbow is to be in the right location at the right time. If you're shooting at a waterfall and don't see a rainbow, walk around to different locations. If the sun is behind you and there is mist in the air, there will be a rainbow nearby.

Exposure—To enhance and dramatize the different colors of the rainbow, underexpose the scene by about one exposure step. This saturates the colors of the rainbow. Don't worry about underexposing the surrounding scene. A slightly dark background often enhances the rainbow and gives the scene a dramatic appearance.

Rainbow Filter—Special filters are available that superimpose an artificial rainbow on a scene. Use these filters with caution. We prefer to use them only in situations where a real rainbow is feasible. For example, we would never include a rainbow in backlit scene. A real rainbow would not occur in such conditions and the picture would look phony.

PEOPLE

Waterfalls are a great location for pictures of people.

Large Falls—At large waterfalls, such as Niagara Falls, you may find catwalks built practically under the falls. Visitors, dressed in bright yellow slickers, get a chance to experience the power and beauty of the falls from this unique vantage point. To capture close-ups of these intrepid people taking a natural shower, you may need a telephoto lens in the 100-200mm range.

We've taken full-frame shots of people at Niagara Falls with our telephoto lenses. However, we also photographed the same scene from the same viewpoint with a wide-angle lens. The resulting picture, which showed the people as small yellow specks, captured the tremendous size and power of the falls.

Small Falls—Small waterfalls are great for in-water portraits. A photograph of a friend under a waterfall, with the water bouncing off his head, will capture the refreshing feeling of being in the cool, clear water.

Interesting pictures can also be taken from behind a waterfall. On a trip to the Philippines, we spent a day on the river where *Apocalypse Now* was filmed. At the end of the river was a small waterfall. With the camera sealed in a waterproof housing, we swam under the falls. Once safely behind the falls, we took a picture of our guide silhouetted against a beautiful curtain of water.

If you are going to swim under waterfalls, we recommend that you secure your camera in a floating plastic underwater housing. If your camera accidentally gets knocked out of your hand by the force of the water, you're more likely to retrieve it if it floats than if it sinks.

A beautiful composition, shot in Arizona's Grand Canyon area. The waterfall occupies a small part of the image area but still dominates the scene. The human-interest foreground lends scale to the scene. Photo by Scott Millard.

RIVERS

Living close to a river, as we do, has many advantages. One is that we have the opportunity to photograph the ever-changing view. Some days, huge commercial fishing boats pass by, followed by dozens of hungry sea gulls. At weekends, the river is filled with small sailboats and motorboats. Activities on the river bank, such as fishing, volleyball and picnicking, are also fun to photograph.

GLARE AND SPARKLE

On a sunny day, when you are facing toward the sun, you will see a beautiful sparkle on the water of a river.

Glare and sparkle can be reduced with a polarizing filter. Rotate the filter on the lens until you see the result you want in the viewfinder. However, before you take a picture, ask yourself whether you really want to remove *all* the glare and reflection. Often, if you remove all the highlights from a water scene, the picture will look very dull.

If you've had any doubt that blurred waterfalls look better than "frozen" ones, these two pictures should convince you. For the left photo, the shutter speed was 1/250 second. The right photo was made at a shutter speed of 1/15 second—long enough to blur and streak the running water. Doesn't the right picture look more like a real waterfall? Remember to use a tripod with the slow shutter speeds, or *everything* in the scene may be blurred!

Seeing Through Water—By eliminating the sun's reflection and any other reflection on the water, you may be able to capture part of the underwater scene. This can result in a photograph showing underwater vegetation, fish or moss-covered rocks.

Hot Spots—Rivers and streams often feature wet rocks protruding from them or at their banks. When sunlight is reflected from these toward the camera, harsh glare can result. To eliminate these *hot spots,* which wash out color and detail, you can use a polarizing filter. Rotate the filter on the camera lens until you see the image you want.

Starbursts—A star filter turns points of light into beautiful starbursts. When photographing scenes with sparkle on the water, this filter can add a magical touch to the photograph.

The more small highlights there are on the water, the more stars you'll have in your photograph. Filters are available to produce anything from two-pointed to 16-pointed stars. We like to use filters producing four-pointed or eight-pointed stars. The 16-pointed star pattern tends to make a scene look too confusing.

Star patterns are most effective against a dark background, where the bright streaks of light stand out more clearly.

You can rotate star filters on the lens, so you can control the position of the streaks of light. Always check the position of the starbursts carefully. For example, try to avoid having a bright streak of light shooting through a subject's head.

SMALL BOATS

If you really want to capture the fun and feeling of a day on the river, you'll have to get on a boat. At close range, you can capture a person's expression and involvement in his activity. For example, you can photograph a rower, straining at the oars of a small rowboat. Or, you can photograph

With a 16mm fisheye lens, Susan was able to shoot this photo while in the boat, just a couple of feet from Rick. She was able to include much of the boat, the oars and a lot of background. If she had wanted to keep the horizon line flat, she would have had to place it in the center of the frame.

a pretty maiden relaxing on the deck of a small motorboat or sailboat.

Here are a few tips for shooting in small boats:

Protect Your Equipment—A plastic bag, with a hole cut out for the lens, will protect your camera from splashes. Film and accessories should also be well protected.

Wide-Angle Lens—When you shoot people on board, use a wide-angle lens. We use 16mm, 17mm, 24mm and 35mm lenses.

A 16mm lens has a very wide angle of view. If you're not careful, you may get your feet in the picture. Check the bottom of the frame before you shoot. Depth of field is almost unlimited.

When we want more of the subject to fill the frame, we shoot with a 24mm or 35mm lens. These lenses allow us to get head-to-toe portraits in most situations.

Backlighting—Subjects on boats are often backlit, either by a bright sky or by sunlight reflected from the water. Unless you want a silhouette, take a close-up meter reading of your subject. If you can't, use the +1 or +2 setting on your exposure compensation dial to compensate for the backlight.

Polarizing Filter—This filter can darken a blue sky and highlight white clouds for a more dramatic image. It can also reduce or even eliminate glare on the water.

Nude photography can be fun, but it isn't easy. A good photo demands careful posing, appropriate lighting and the right background. In this area of photography as in no other, the difference between an excellent and a dreadful photo can be very slight. Allow your model to be part of the creative process. Direct her, but give her a chance to use her own ideas and poses, too. Photo by Lucien Clergue.

SHORELINE

The ocean shoreline offers an infinite variety of picture-taking opportunities. We've taken pictures of waves crashing on stone jetties, with spray rising 15 feet or more in the air. We have photographed fishing villages, complete with old fishing boats.

Shooting candid people pictures and environmental portraits at the shoreline is also fun and challenging. In natural surroundings, people tend to be more at ease than in the formal atmosphere of a portrait studio.

FOG AND MIST

Fog and mist subdue colors, reduce contrast and blur detail. If you shoot through mist, your photographs will often look more like paintings. Boats, people and buildings take on an ethereal glow in light fog. An old fishing boat may look like a ghost ship lost at sea.

Avoid heavy fog, in which visibility is very poor. Photographic images will be equally poor.

Adding Fog—If weather conditions are crystal clear and you want to take "mist" pictures, don't despair. You can use a fog or mist filter to add artificial fog to a scene. These filters are available in several grades, so you can select your own fog density. The filters work well. However, even with the strongest filter you may still see shadows and highlights in your images. Also, you won't be able to selectively "fog out" a distracting background.

DOCKSIDE

Whether you're at a fishing village, historic marine park or waterfront town, you can always find people engaged in some activity at dockside.

Fishing Villages—When fishing boats come in after a day at sea, you can get interesting pictures of fishermen unloading their catch from huge nets and baskets. And there's no doubt that sea gulls will be in the background looking for a handout. It can be effective to give a picture of this kind an antique look by using a sepia filter with color-slide film. The picture will look like an old brown-tone photo.

This harbor scene in Sicily consisted almost entirely of foreground interest. However, the photographer carefully framed the scene to also include the distant horizon, mountains and sky. Photo by Lou Jones.

To photograph illuminated night scenes, use fast film and a tripod. It's advisable to use daylight-balanced film. It records tungsten illumination with its characteristic warm, orange glow.

Historic Marine Parks—Waterfront parks, complete with square riggers, small fishing boats and quaint old buildings, are good locations for scenic photography. These settings are also an excellent background for people pictures. Here you may see "characters" dressed in costumes of the period. These people are usually very cooperative. Try photographing them engaged in some interesting activity, such as rigging a sail or hauling an anchor line.

AFTER DARK

You don't have to put your camera away when the sun goes down. You can shoot late into the evening, to get striking images of lighted docks, riverside cafes, bridges and city skyscrapers—and their reflections in water. A good time to shoot is at dusk, when lights are already lit but there's still a glow of daylight in the sky.

You can also get attractive pictures of people at spotlight-illuminated docks or piers.

Film—We generally use daylight-balanced ISO 400/27° color-slide film for our nighttime pictures of water scenery. It is fast enough for low light levels and reproduces tungsten illumination with an attractive reddish, "warm" glow.

When photographing people illuminated by spot or flood lamps, we prefer tungsten-balanced color-slide film. It reproduces skin tone in its natural color.

If you want to use the same film for all your nighttime photography, we recommend the daylight-balanced film. For photographing the lights, use no filter. For portraiture, use a bluish filter in the 80 or 82 series to get accurate skin-tone rendition.

Exposure—A typical exposure for a waterfront scene shortly after sunset with ISO 400/27° film is about 1/30 second at *f*-5.6. With ISO 200/24° film, a good starting exposure is 1/30 second at *f*-4. Recommended starting exposures for nighttime photography are supplied with most high-speed 35mm films. To ensure satisfactory photos in a variety of conditions, bracket your exposures.

Exposure times of several seconds or even minutes streak the moving lights of boats in a picture. These streaks can add a dramatic touch to your nighttime water-scenery pictures. Exposure will vary with the intensity of the lights and your distance from them. Take a reading of the scene and bracket a full two *f*-stops under and over the recommended setting. This should ensure a pleasing photo.

Tripod and Cable Release—For long exposures, you'll need a sturdy tripod to support your camera. It's also advisable to use a cable release, which enables you to release the shutter without touching the camera body.

To the observant photographer, nature offers not only fine backgrounds but also many natural props. For this picture, the photographer made excellent use of a rock formation for posing his model. Photo by Harry Benson.

To blur the waterfall, a shutter speed of 1/30 second was used. However, that exposure time would also have blurred the falling subject. By waiting until the man was at the highest point in his swing, it was possible to record him sharply because he was almost static in midair. Photo by Charles Basham.

Mist and light fog are useful tools for creating the feeling of distance. The nearby boat and its occupants are clear and have good contrast. The mountains in the distance are barely visible through the bluish haze.

6 Water Sports

You'll find people engaged in water sports at lakes, rivers, streams, pools and the ocean. The activities you can see and photograph include swimming, diving, sailing, speed-boat racing, water skiing and many others. Sometimes you may witness professionals testing their skills in fierce competition. Other subjects may be weekend athletes who just enjoy being on the water.

In some cases, you'll photograph an activity from dry land. At other times, you may follow the action from an accompanying boat. Or, you may be on the same vessel where the action is.

After a few practice sessions, you'll be prepared to capture the fast-paced action of virtually any water sport.

Canada 1 giving its best during the America's Cup preliminary races off Newport, Rhode Island. A dramatic head-on view of a rapidly approaching vessel is possible only with a long telephoto lens. Photo by Lou Jones.

SWIMMING

Our best advice on photographing swimmers is to take lots of pictures. A swimmer changes his position and expression constantly. One moment he's facing this way and the next moment that way. Sometimes his head is submerged. At times, his expression is less than photogenic.

A motor drive is invaluable. Use one to take rapid picture sequences. Then select the best shots at your leisure after the film is processed.

Above Water—To capture the excitement a swimmer feels as he glides through the water, shoot from water level. You can lie on your stomach at the side of the pool. Shoot side views of a swimmer passing you and frontal views of a swimmer heading toward you. To freeze the action on film, use a fast shutter speed—1/500 second or 1/1000 second.

To get even closer to the water level, get into the water with your camera. Hold the camera just above the water. Protect the camera in a suitable plastic underwater housing, as discussed in the *Equipment* chapter, page 4.

Under Water—Swimmers make interesting underwater subjects. Especially the turns at the ends of the pool can make for exciting pictures. Take side-view shots as a swimmer reaches the wall, turns and pushes off again.

To see clearly under water, you'll need a face mask or swimming goggles. The camera equipment needn't be elaborate. The "fun" cameras described in the *Equipment* chapter, page 4, will do fine.

Competition—When shooting competitive swimming events, get several swimmers into the picture. Show the strain and concentration in their faces and their bodily movements. Get a high view to show clearly the progress of each swimmer in his lane. Concentrate on just one swimmer for some of your photos.

DIVING

Much of the fun and action at swimming pools is around diving boards. Here's some useful advice: When a non-expert dives, he usually looks better in real life than in a photo. That's because the actual dive happens so fast that you don't see the details. Only when various stages are recorded on film, where you can study them at your leisure, does the awkwardness of the dive become evident.

If you want impressive diving pictures, photograph an impressive diver!

Stopping Action—To arrest subject movement on film, we use a 1/1000-second shutter speed. We generally take diving photos on fast film—Ektachrome 400 for color slides and Kodacolor VR 400 for color prints. Indoors, we use the same films with electronic flash.

Second Try—Divers often repeat the same dive several times. Begin by observing the diver a few times. Then select the moment in the dive when you think you'll get the best shot. Usually, you'll get the most impressive picture just after the diver leaves the board, when he reaches the peak of the action between ascent and descent, and just as he enters the water.

Sequences—We like to shoot sequences, from the moment the diver starts from the diving board to his disappearance in the water. We achieve this with a motor drive capable of a 3.5-frames-per-second speed. At this operating speed, we can get nearly a dozen shots of one dive. Before you shoot fast sequences, be sure you have enough film left in the camera.

Background—The blue sky, unobstructed by telephone poles, wires or trees, makes an ideal background for diving pictures. This calls for a low viewpoint, which also makes a dive look more impressive.

When selecting your position for photographing a dive, visualize the entire arc of the dive. This way you'll be sure you don't have a distracting background when the diver is in the most impressive position.

Compositionally, the diver is in an excellent location in relationship with the other picture elements. His body position is graceful—indicating a skillful diver and an alert photographer. The low viewpoint toward the towering, silhouetted diving platforms adds excitement to the picture. The spotlighting of the diver against the sun adds drama. Photo by Theodore DiSante.

Even a photo of one lone swimmer can effectively depict competitive swimming. This man is obviously not swimming for relaxation. He means business—keeping ahead of those behind him and catching those ahead. Photo from Focus on Sports, Inc.

Different Viewpoints—You can photograph divers from just about anywhere around a pool. Try shooting from the side, the front, from the water and even from the back of the diving board. Get close-up studies of a diver's action with a telephoto lens. Then use a wide-angle lens to record the diver and his environment.

If there's a tall building nearby, you may be able to get a good general view from one of the upper floors.

Multiple Dives—You can get impressive photos of two or more divers descending together. It's best to get the cooperation of the divers. Talk to them in advance and tell them what you want. If you promise each diver a print or slide of the result, they'll usually be delighted to help.

Try shooting multiple dives with experts only. A picture of three bad divers will probably be at least three times as bad as a picture of one! And the feat could be dangerous, too.

To take effective sailing pictures, keep the horizon horizontal at all times, regardless of how the boat is tilting. Photo by Jake Grubb.

SAILING

Sailboats come in many sizes, colors and shapes. You'll find them on lakes and rivers and on the ocean. You may see experts competing for trophies at impressive speeds. Or, you may witness weekend sailors, out for a leisurely Sunday afternoon.

Following are some guidelines for photographing sailing events:

Back Light—Back lighting has three important effects on sailboat pictures: It provides sparkling reflections from the water. Illumination from behind sails makes their colors stand out brilliantly. And, back lighting causes the boat and its occupants to be recorded in silhouette or semi-silhouette.

To get the exact effect you want, it's advisable to bracket exposures liberally. Under backlit conditions, a meter will not always indicate the exposure that will give the most impressive image.

Horizon Line—When a boat is sailing at top speed and tilting with the wind, keep the horizon horizontal and record the boat at a tilt. That way you'll capture the action most convincingly. A picture wouldn't look right with the boat upright and the horizon tilted.

Remember this advice especially if you're on the boat you're photographing. It's easy to be tempted to always keep the boat upright.

Action—The most spectacular action shots are those in which the sails are filled with wind. Without this evidence of wind and motion, sailboat pictures look static.

On-Board Pictures—You can get great pictures of a sailboat crew in action. For on-board "environmental" portraits, we use wide-angle lenses ranging from 17mm to 35mm. These lenses enable us to get the subject and much of the boat in the picture. Wide-angle lenses also provide great depth of field.

With a 17mm lens, we can get the subject, deck and part of the sails into one photograph. A 35mm lens is suitable for more detailed portraits that still include some background.

If you're on a boat that has a sturdy main mast, complete with rope ladder, you can climb to the top and shoot downward with a wide-angle lens. With a 17mm, 20mm or 24mm lens, your picture will include boat and surrounding water. The wide-angle lens will also have the dramatic effect of making the mast appear much taller than it actually is.

Climb the mast only with the captain's approval—and only if you feel comfortable at heights on a moving and bobbing vessel!

WATER SKIING

The best viewpoint for taking action pictures of water skiers is from the tow boat. If you shoot from the shore, your subject will be relatively small in the viewfinder, even if you use a telephoto lens. Also, from the shore you'll miss most of the drama of the wake of the boat and the spray created by the skier.

Lenses—On a speed boat, you'll bounce up and down as the boat braves the waves. In our experience, it's unwise to use a telephoto lens of 300mm or longer. The motion and vibration of the boat can cause blurred pictures, even when you use a shutter speed of 1/1000 second. The bouncing around also makes it difficult to compose the scene in the viewfinder with a very long lens.

We use a 200mm lens for full-frame shots of water skiers. By using a 1/1000-second shutter speed and concentrating on framing the image, it's possible to make good pictures with this lens. We also use wide-angle lenses to capture in one picture the water skier, tow rope and the water pattern created by the motion.

Focus—When the tow rope is taught, the camera-to-subject distance remains the same. You don't have to refocus as the skier swings back and forth across the wake. You can concentrate your entire attention on the action and picture composition.

Spray and Wake—From the back of the boat you'll see the wake of the boat and the spray created by the skier. The faster the boat, the higher the trail of spray the boat and skier leave behind. In photos, the spray accentuates the speed of the water skier.

Back lighting highlights and emphasizes the spray. Because water skiers generally go around in large circles, you'll have the benefit of lighting from many directions during your shooting.

In this photo, you don't see water or even a boat. But it's still a dynamic sailing picture. The sail is full and the crew is active. Photo by Lou Jones.

The water itself forms an important part of the composition of many water-skiing pictures. Focus on the skier once and then forget focusing—the skier will always be the tow-rope length away from the boat. Concentrate on getting the wake and the spray just right for an impressive composition.

Photographing a free-moving jet skier is a little more difficult that shooting a water skier at the end of a tow rope. You have to refocus as the distance between you and the skier changes. This is especially true when you're using a telephoto lens, which gives limited depth of field.

Plan your photography carefully. But be prepared for the unexpected, too. A spill, with all the accompanying spray, can make for a dramatic action picture. Photo by Patricia Caulfield.

Spills—Sooner or later most water skiers fall. Sometimes they do it gracefully and unspectacularly, sinking slowly into the water. At other times, they hit the wake of the boat and do a spectacular flip before crashing into the water. Be alert, so you don't miss those moments.

Accessories—We habitually use a motor drive when photographing water skiers. If you use one, take along plenty of film. Shooting fast-paced action with a motor drive quickly uses up film. We also protect the camera in a plastic bag, to keep it dry.

Secure Your Camera—A final tip on shooting from a power boat: Use the camera strap. At high speed, you'll get bounced around—sometimes suddenly and violently. If your camera is securely around your neck, there's less danger of it joining the skier in the water!

JET SKIING

Jet skis are motorized, self-propelled water skis. The exciting sport of jet skiing has become very popular in recent years. Many resort and beach-front hotels offer it as an activity. Guests can rent a jet ski for half an hour or an hour at a modest price. You'll also find jet skiers at marinas and boat ramps.

In some water sports, you must follow the action. In others, it's better to wait for the action to come to you. Rafting is a typical example of the latter. Position yourself near turbulent rapids—and be prepared. That's where the thrills, and spills, will occur. Photo by Patricia Caulfield.

Would you call this surfboard riding or water skiing? Either way, this "surfboard skier" is having fun.

Jet skis can travel at 25 miles per hour, so capturing the action takes planning and practice.

Subject Cooperation—To get the best pictures, you need the help and cooperation of the jet skier. Generally, he will want a picture of the occasion as much as you do. Promise him one, and you'll be on your way.

Discuss the details of the ride with the subject. Ask him to pass back and forth as close to the shore as possible. If he's about 30 feet from the beach, you can get good, detailed shots with a 200mm or 300mm telephoto lens.

For a spectacular shot, ask the subject to do a quick 360° turn in which he'll throw up a curtain of spray.

To accentuate the speed of a jet skier, use the *panning* technique described in the *Water Shows* chapter, page 65.

Beach Landing—The subject may be willing to ride the jet ski onto the sand. This is a common way of finishing a ride. Just before he reaches the sand, you have a chance of shooting a frontal view, with ocean in the background.

If you suggest a beach landing, be sure the skier has done it before. Don't encourage him to take risks for the sake of your pictures.

RAFT RIDING

Raft riding on rivers is popular in many parts of the country. Some do it in expensive rubber rafts, specially designed to negotiate rough water. Others use old inner tubes.

Viewpoint—The key to getting good pictures of raft riders is to find a position near turbulent rapids. This is where the exciting action is. Here, you'll see your subjects pick up speed, go through hair-raising maneuvers, and sometimes lose control and have a "spill."

A bridge over a river can provide a good shooting location. Shooting from a low bridge with a long telephoto lens, you can get head-on photographs. These pictures place the viewer right in the middle of the action. You may even be able to see the excitement in the riders' faces.

Seasonal Sport—In mountainous areas where melting snow affects water volume, raft riding is seasonal. In the early Spring, when the snow melts, the water level is generally at its peak. This is when the rapids are raging. It's the high season for raft riding. By early summer, the water level in many rivers starts to drop. By Fall, the raft-riding season is over in many areas. Specific information can be found in brochures available from raft-riding concessions.

Many of the best water photographs are shot against the light. This is a good example. The ripple created by the boat on the smooth water is highlighted. There's little detail of the boat—but the silhouetted oars tell the story very effectively. Photo by Lou Jones.

About the only location from which you can get dramatic head-on shots like this of rowers is from a bridge. To avoid getting a top view, use a telephoto lens and shoot when the boat is at a reasonable distance from the bridge. Photo by Lou Jones.

The airborne boat has just left a ramp. To capture the action, Rick prefocused on the ramp. When the boat appeared in the desired location in the viewfinder, Rick made the exposure. The shutter speed was 1/1000 second. At 1/500 second, you may get some image blur with this kind of subject.

SURFING

For exciting surfing pictures, you need a good surf—the higher the better.

Surfers generally ride waves that break fairly far off shore. This means you'll have to use a long lens—maybe 400mm or even 500mm—to get detailed photographs. Our equipment for shooting surfers regularly includes a 100-500mm telephoto zoom lens. It enables us to frame the fast-moving surfers quickly and accurately.

We use a monopod to support the camera and help reduce the danger of camera shake.

Focus—A long telephoto lens has very limited depth of field. To keep a fast-moving surfer in sharp focus, you'll need to refocus constantly. Doing this fast takes a little practice. You may want to try it out in your neighborhood on moving cars, bicycles or joggers—with an unloaded camera.

BEHIND THE SCENES

Not all great sports photos are taken while the subject is on or in the water. For example, you can get interesting pictures of sailors preparing to leave port, surfers waxing their surfboards or jet skiers giving their machines a tune-up. You can record on film a subject's exciting anticipation of an event or his exhaustion at the end of strenuous activity.

7 Photographing Animals

Many wild animals and birds live near a water environment. Around ponds and lakes you may find ducks, geese, frogs and turtles. By the riverside you may see beavers and even bears. At the seashore you'll have the company of many species of birds. In southern marsh areas, there are alligators and other reptiles. Almost all bodies of water abound in fish.

Zoos and wildlife parks are excellent places to photograph captive animals, especially if you've never taken animal photographs before. Get some experience at the zoo, before you venture into the great outdoors.

In a zoo or wildlife park, the animals are usually in a simulated natural habitat. You'll see polar bears in big outdoor pens, complete with a pool of cool water. Birds are often in large walk-in aviaries. In these, you'll always find a pond or two. Sea lions have a pool of their own and lions and tigers, too, have their own watering holes.

Photography at aquariums is discussed on page 68, in the chapter on *Water Shows,* so we won't say more about it here.

We have divided this chapter into two parts. The section on *Wildlife* covers photography in the great outdoors. The *Captive Animals* section tells you how to take pictures at zoos and other animal parks.

This photo was planned well. The shot was made at sunrise. A long telephoto lens was used to get a large image of the sun. The photographer positioned himself so two of the birds were silhouetted against the sun's reflection. Photo by Lucien Clergue.

WILDLIFE

Photographing animals in their wild state is challenging. It can also be a rewarding experience, if you have the proper equipment and some understanding of your subject's habits and ways.

EQUIPMENT

Having the right equipment can make the difference between a spectacular photo and a mere snapshot. *Always* carry the right equipment for the job. *Never* carry more than necessary. Following is the equipment we use:

Two Camera Bodies—With two camera bodies, we can have two lenses of different focal lengths ready for instant use. We can shoot a detailed animal portrait with a 300mm lens. In seconds, we can switch to a 100mm lens for a photo that includes more of the animal plus some background.

We can also load each camera with a different film type. One can contain ISO 400/27° high-speed film for shooting in shaded areas.

Rick managed to shoot this submerged frog in a pleasing composition of floating leaves. Exact focus on the most important part—the frog's eye—was essential.

The second camera can be loaded with ISO 64/19° medium-speed film for photographing in bright sunlight.

Telephoto Lenses—For photographing wild animals, we believe telephoto lenses in the 100mm to 400mm range are essential. With a 2X converter, the effective focal lengths of these lenses can be doubled. For example, a 400mm lens on a 2X converter effectively gives you an 800mm lens.

Telephoto Zoom—In wild-animal photography, you can expect the camera-to-subject distance to change almost constantly. A telephoto zoom lens makes it easy to frame the subject exactly as you want it. We like to use a 100-500mm telephoto zoom. It enables us to change quickly from a general view with background detail to a close-up head shot. It also makes it easy to keep the animal framed properly as it moves about.

A 75-200mm zoom with 2X converter gives an effective focal-length range of 150- 400mm. This represents a good all-around lens for animal photography.

Macro Lens—This is useful for photographing small creatures. Frogs, for example, stay perfectly still to avoid detection. If you step lightly, you can get as close as three or four inches from the frog. A 100mm macro lens will give a greater lens-to-subject distance than a 50mm macro lens, at the same image magnification.

Wide-Angle Lens—Photographing flocks of birds or herds of animals sometimes requires a wide angle of view. We always carry a 28mm lens in our camera bag, just in case such a situation occurs.

Motor Drive or Auto Winder—Wild animals tend to change position constantly. To capture them at their best, use a motor drive or auto winder. With some motor drives you can automatically shoot up to 10 frames per second. Auto winders are designed to automatically advance the film without making the exposures. They can generally advance film at a rate of two frames per second.

Film—When using telephoto lenses, we like to use fast ISO 400/27° film. It enables us to use the camera handheld at a fast shutter speed, eliminating the danger of picture blur due to camera movement. Fast film is also useful for shooting in shaded areas and in early morning or late afternoon. We also carry ISO 64/19° medium-speed film for shooting in bright sunlight and with shorter-focal-length lenses.

Tripod—Unless we need to travel really light, we like to have a tripod with us. When possible, it's always best to use the camera on a tripod when shooting with long telephoto lenses. With a smoothly operating pan-and-tilt head, you can easily keep the camera aimed at even a fast-moving animal.

CLOTHING

The less you're seen, the more you'll achieve photographically. Many animals are naturally camouflaged. You can learn from them. Wear clothing that blends with the environment. Dark green or brown are suitable colors for most outdoor locations.

Waterproof boots are important. You may get your best photographs by walking through water for a good viewpoint. Also, the land surrounding bodies of water is often damp. We wear fishing boots that come up over our knees. They allow us to wade at will without getting wet and uncomfortable.

Commercially-made *shooting vests* and *shooting jackets,* with pockets for lenses, filters, film and camera-cleaning kit, are helpful when you're stalking wild animals. With lenses and accessories at your fingertips, you won't miss an unrepeatable shot because you're fumbling in your camera bag.

HABITS AND CHARACTERISTICS

Most animals are creatures of habit. They sleep, awaken, hunt and feed at about the same times each day. Each species has its own diet. Animals also have their own special characteristics. Some are slow; others are fast. Some see well; others don't. Some have a keen sense of smell. Some are timid; others are daring.

You'll find it easier to locate and photograph animals, if you know something about their traits and "personalities." You can find useful information from leading nature magazines.

For detailed information, get one of the *Petersen Field Guide* series, published by Houghton Mifflin, Boston. These books offer excellent information on where to find animals and what to expect from them. The guides feature full-color drawings. Seasonal maps show when you can expect to encounter your chosen subject. Following are a few of the Petersen guides you may find useful:

- *A Field Guide to Birds*
- *A Field Guide to Mammals*
- *A Field Guide to Reptiles and Amphibians*
- *A Field Guide to Insects of North America*

A little preliminary study *at home* can make things much easier for you out *in the field.*

Exposing a white bird against a dark background can be difficult. You can use an averaging meter and decrease the indicated exposure by 1-1/2 to 2 steps. Or, you can use a spot meter on the bird. This bird, photographed in India, was spot-metered while on the ground. The photographer knew that the bird would remain in the same light when he took off. To get a well-exposed and well-composed shot of this kind calls for silent and rapid action. Photo by John Isaac.

STALKING

Most wild creatures avoid people. If they see you splashing and tramping toward them, they are likely to dash off. This applies to animals, birds, fish and reptiles alike. If you move slowly and unobtrusively and step lightly, you'll have a better chance of getting close. Take your time! Be patient!

The less you disturb the environment, the less an animal will sense that someone is around. Most animals have a keen sense of hearing and smell. Don't talk unnecessarily. Don't smoke and avoid wearing strong cologne or perfume. It also helps to be downwind from the animal.

If you are stalking a wild animal and it spots you, stop immediately and squat down low. The less of you there is to see, the less likely the animal is to run away.

Always remember that wild animals are *wild*—they can be dangerous. Bears can suddenly charge. Alligators can not only snap, but can also do serious damage with their tails. Numerous animals will bite when provoked. Others can poison you. While you enjoy the presence of the animals, always be aware of their less pleasant aspects, too.

ACTION PHOTOS

With wild creatures, you must be on the alert for sudden movements and lucky breaks that may give you a great action photo. For example, assume you are stalking a deer that is taking a drink by a river bank. If it hears or senses you, it'll dash off. Don't think you have lost your chance. The deer will probably create a path of splashes through the water. If you're ready to shoot, you can get a great action photo. Take the following steps to be prepared for action photography:

Have Camera Ready—With the camera turned on and held at chest level, it only takes an instant to bring it to your eye, aim, focus and shoot.

Appropriate Lens—A telephoto zoom lens lets you compose your pictures accurately and quickly in spite of an animal's movements. If you work with fixed-focal-length lenses, be prepared to switch lenses—or cameras—quickly and quietly.

Check Light Level—Take a meter reading of the area where you expect to photograph the animal. If this is not possible, meter a substitute area in similar illumination. Make sure you can shoot at an aperture that will give sufficient depth of field. Also be sure the shutter speed is fast enough to "freeze" the animal's movement.

Preset Focus—Set your lens for the distance at which you expect to shoot. Be sure you have enough depth of field to allow for movement of the animal without losing sharpness. When you have enough time, refocus when the animal moves away from you or toward you.

Motor Drive or Auto Winder—With one or other of these devices, you can shoot from two to 10 frames per second. The faster you can shoot, the more likely you are to get the "perfect" action photo.

A sea turtle returning to its ocean home. The low viewpoint adds apparent size to the turtle and also presents a pleasing profile. Photo by C. Allan Morgan, Peter Arnold, Inc.

Pelicans make good models. Sometimes, they can be captured on film while diving for fish, just off the coast. At other times, they will pose for you relatively peacefully on the ground, as in this picture. Photo by Charles Basham.

Check Surrounding Area—When you spot an animal, look for an escape route the animal may take. Be prepared to shoot in that direction.

ANIMAL PORTRAITS

Following are some suggestions on how to compose and shoot an animal portrait:

Head and Full-Length Shots—If you shoot with a long telephoto lens or a telephoto zoom, you have the best chance of filling the frame with the subject's head.

When shooting full-length portraits, using a wide lens aperture will put the background slightly out of focus. This makes the subject stand out clearly from the background. For example, if you're shooting a bird on a tree branch, you can deliberately blur other branches and foliage.

Environmental Portraits—To get a good picture, you need not always fill the frame with your subject. By including some surrounding area, you can create an *environmental* portrait. For example, if you are photographing an animal bathing in a river, include an ample section of the river in the picture. If you're photographing a beaver building a dam, include a portion of the dam. In this way your portraits can tell a story about an animal's activities and surroundings.

For environmental photos, you'll generally need a relatively short telephoto lens, perhaps in the 100mm to 200mm range. A 75-200mm telephoto zoom is also suitable.

When the environment tells part of the story, shoot at a small aperture so you get the entire scene in focus. You may need a fast film, such as ISO 200/24° or ISO 400/27°, to achieve this. Before you make the exposure, check the depth-of-field scale on your lens or use the depth-of-field preview button on the camera to check overall image sharpness.

Frame with Grass, Branches or Rocks—You can create a three-dimensional effect by framing the subject with branches, grass, rocks or other natural foregrounds. Aim your camera through the foreground frame. Try to get the animal in the best possible position within the frame. It doesn't matter if the foreground isn't totally sharp. However, it should not be so blurred as to be unrecognizable.

HIDE IN A BLIND

A *blind* is a structure in which you can hide to avoid detection by animals. Patience is the key ingredient for shooting from a blind. You may have to sit in the blind and wait for several hours before an animal comes into view.

Natural Blind—A bush, tall grass, a fallen tree or any natural growth or formation behind which you can hide can constitute a natural blind. If you explore the area where you expect to encounter animals, you'll probably find a hiding place from which you can shoot unnoticed.

Manufactured Blind—If you plan to spend a lot of time on wildlife photography, a commercially made blind may be the best answer. They are available in sporting-goods stores. They're designed specifically for hunters. However, they are just as suitable for "shooting" animals with a camera.

Blinds made for duck shooting are generally of a tan color. For hunting animals, blinds are usually green. The important thing is that the blind is not easily detectable in the surroundings where you place it.

Homemade Blind—You can construct your own blind to suit your specific needs. For a one-person blind, all you need is three five-feet-long bamboo poles, some strong wire and a tarpaulin. Set the bamboo poles up teepee-style.

This charming study of Alaskan brown bears was made with a 600mm lens. It enabled the photographer to stay at a safe distance and at the same time capture the uninhibited behavior of the animals. Photo by Galen Rowell, Peter Arnold, Inc.

Secure them at the top with the wire. Drape the tarpaulin over the teepee. Cut an opening in the tarpaulin for the camera lens. Your blind is complete and you're ready to "move in" and shoot.

Tent—A small tent makes a good blind. It can be carried in a backpack and set up in a few minutes. If you have no luck in one location, you can easily move to another position.

If you buy a tent for a blind, choose a color that'll blend with most natural backgrounds. Gray or a dull green are fine. Avoid bright colors like orange and red. They contrast too sharply with the natural environment.

Car—If you can drive right up to your shooting location, consider using your car as a blind. Keep the window through which you'll shoot open. Remain quiet while you wait.

REMOTE CONTROL

Some animals and birds are so shy that it's impossible to get close enough to photograph them. However, it is possible to capture them on film with the help of a remote-control unit.

A remote-control unit consists of a handheld *transmitter* and a camera-mounted *receiver.* You operate the transmitter to send a signal to the camera, to trigger the shutter.

The unit may be operated by *radio* or through the use of *infrared radiation.* Both trigger the camera from a distance. Some units permit a distance between you and your camera of up to 200 feet.

A simple form of remote control consists of a long cable release. The distance between you and the camera is determined by the length of the cable.

Hiding Location—Find a position that hides you from the animals but allows you a clear view of the shooting area. When using an infrared unit, you need a clear line of view between transmitter and receiver. This is because infrared rays travel in a straight line and will not penetrate solid objects. If you're using a radio-controlled unit, you have more flexibility as to your position. However, you must still be able to see the shooting site.

Provide for Yourself—Once you are in your hiding spot, it may be several hours before your subject comes into view. Therefore, you must be prepared for a long wait. Have patience. Be alert. Keep quiet. And, provide for yourself. Take some food, plenty of drinking water, and clothing appropriate to the weather conditions.

Other Accessories—When you are shooting with a remote-control unit, you'll need a motor drive or auto winder to advance the film. Otherwise, you would have to walk back to the camera to advance the film after each exposure. You'll also need a sturdy tripod for the camera.

Camera Setup—Mount your camera on the tripod and focus on the anticipated subject position. Make sure the camera setup can't be knocked over by a passing animal. Cover the tripod with

With skill and luck, you can take zoo pictures that look as if they might have been taken in the wild. There's no "maybe" about this one. This moose is obviously enjoying the vast expanse of its natural home. Photo by Steven Fuller, Peter Arnold, Inc.

foliage or grass, to hide it from the animals' view.

When you aim the camera, be sure there is no unwanted clutter within view. This could include beer bottles or cans on the ground or telephone poles in the background.

Exposure—Be sure your shutter is set to a fast enough speed to record a moving animal sharply. Also, use a lens aperture that will give enough depth of field to get the entire subject in focus. You can't determine exactly how far the animal will be from the camera when you shoot. Therefore, you need some extra "insurance" depth of field.

Attract the Animals—You can lure animals to your shooting position with food or a decoy. Birds like bread and seed. Different kinds of seeds attract different bird species. Frogs will also eat bread. If you sprinkle a few large crumbs on the surface of a pond, a hungry frog may eventually arrive on the scene. On the other hand, he may not!

Deer can be attracted to water areas with a salt lick, available at grain and feed stores. If you can't obtain a salt lick, a mound of salt will do.

Ducks like company. You can purchase special decoys at hunting-equipment stores. Place a decoy in the water. If there are ducks in the area, they will come. You can also lure ducks with bread.

You can find more information on the diets of animals and birds in the *Petersen Field Guides,* mentioned earlier in this chapter.

CAPTIVE ANIMALS

Animals and birds that naturally live near water are provided with a water environment in zoos and animal parks, too. Creatures in captivity are usually easier to photograph than those in the wilderness. You can get fairly close to them, because they are confined and are accustomed to people. These animals are fed regularly and generally come to a specific location for their meals.

To photograph captive animals, you can use much of the equipment and many of the shooting techniques discussed earlier in this chapter. However, there are a few new tips and techniques you should know, before you leave home.

OBSTACLES

Zoos present certain obstacles that can make getting the picture you want difficult. Generally, you don't want bars or a wire fence to appear in your pictures. You can make them disappear in one of two ways.

You can place the camera lens close to the barrier and aim between the bars or the wire mesh. However, you can only do this when you have close access to the barrier and when the animal is not likely to strike out at the camera.

The second way is to throw the barrier sufficiently out of focus to become totally invisible. With a long-focal-length lens, a wide lens aperture and a short distance between camera and barrier, you have the best chance of achieving this. Focus on the subject, which should be several feet behind the barrier. The bars or wire will then be so much out of focus as to be totally undetectable in the photo.

If you specifically want to *include* bars or fences sharply in your pictures, use a shorter-focal-length lens. Stand well back from the obstacle and shoot at a small lens aperture.

CROWDS

On a busy day, a zoo contains more people than animals. These fellow visitors can often get in your way. Before you shoot, make sure nobody is about to run in front of your camera. When you set up your camera on a tripod, make sure someone is watching it all the time. It could easily be knocked over by the passing crowd.

The closer you place your camera to the animal's compound or pen, the less room there will be for people to pass in front of you.

People Pictures—You can also make *good* use of the people at the zoo in your photography. You can get great shots of the reaction of children when they see a strange animal for the first time. Try to get both the child and the animal into the picture.

At petting areas, you can photograph children and animals together. If you're within a few feet of the subject, you can use a wide-angle lens in the 24mm to 35mm range. If you're on the far side of pool, cage or pen, you may need a telephoto lens.

FEEDING TIME

You're likely to get your best photographs at feeding times. During these periods, you'll see more animal activity than at any other time. Details of feeding times should be available at the zoo or park information desk. Or, these times may be posted near each animal's pool, cage or pen.

Check the feeding times as soon as you get to the zoo. Then you'll know where to be at what times.

Two unlikely friends. To record a moment like this, you have to be alert to the ever-changing scene about you. And, use a long lens, keep your distance, and stay quiet. Photo by Edward Slater, Southern Stock Photos.

Animals are very active just before feeding time. You'll see them pacing back and forth, jumping and running while awaiting the attendant's arrival.

SHOOTING FROM A CAR

In wildlife parks, you can photograph wild animals from the comfort and safety of your car. You can take all the equipment you want, without worrying about lugging it about all day. Here are a few tips for getting the best from your mobile-studio photography.

Be a Passenger—It's difficult to concentrate on photography while you're driving a car. Have a companion drive. You can give directions as to when to stop and when to go.

Shooting Through Glass—Most wildlife parks insist that you keep your windows closed at all times. The park management doesn't want you feeding, petting or playing with animals that may harm you. Before you enter the animal area, be sure the car windows are thoroughly clean.

When shooting through glass, hold the lens close to the window. If you don't, you may also record on film unwanted reflections from the inside surface of the window.

You can hold the lens in contact with the window, as long as the car engine is switched off. With the engine running, vibration from the window could be transferred to the camera, causing camera shake. This could lead to blurred pictures. A rubber lens hood on the lens can be helpful. When held against the window, the rubber will absorb most of the vibration from a running car.

Try to avoid shooting through the front and back windows. Their curvature and angle may distort the image.

RESPECT ALL CREATURES

Whether you are photographing wild or tame animals, respect them and think of their wellbeing. Don't taunt or tease. Don't feed them if you are asked not to or if you don't know what might harm them. There's no satisfaction in taking home a prize-winning photograph when you know you may have harmed the animal in the process of making it.

8 Photography at the Pool

Swimming pools are everywhere—at plush resorts, in cities and in private backyards or homes. When it's indoors or heated, a pool can be used during the whole year. Many picture-taking possibilities exist in and around pools.

GLAMOUR

Professional photographers often use a swimming pool as the setting for fashion and glamour photography. Pools are popular because they are associated with a youthful lifestyle and convey a feeling of fun and freedom. You, too, can use a swimming-pool setting for this kind of photography.

Many of the basics of glamour photography have been discussed already in the *Shooting at the Beach* chapter. You can apply these to your pool-side photography. Following are some additional tips.

Privacy—Your subject will feel much more comfortable if there aren't alot of people watching while you're shooting. An uncrowded pool is better for you, too, because you have more freedom in selecting a background.

If you're going to shoot at a public or resort pool, find out in advance when it's least crowded. When possible, shoot at a private pool.

Lighting—As we've explained earlier, the best lighting for people pictures is when the sun is low in the sky. Try to shoot early or late in the day. Be aware, however, that many pools are surrounded by buildings that can cause the pool to be in shade at those times. Check in advance when the lighting conditions are best at the pool you've selected.

A swimming pool is an excellent location for underwater pictures. This scene was illuminated by overhead sunlight. The light-blue pool bottom acted as a reflector, brightening the shadows below the swimmer. Use fast film. You need the fastest shutter speed and the smallest lens aperture possible. Photo by Werner J. Bertsch, Southern Stock Photos.

Props—Make use of the many effective props you find around pools. The poses you can photograph are limited only by your imagination. Have your model lie on a diving board, stand against a lifeguard stand, sip a tall, cool drink at a table with a colorful umbrella or recline in a lounge chair.

To make the subject's body glisten in the sun, have her apply suntan lotion uniformly over her body.

You'll find additional useful information and glamour photographs in *Pro Techniques of People Photography* and *How to Photograph Women,* both published by HPBooks.

UNDER WATER

If you've never taken underwater photographs, a swimming pool is the perfect place to start. You can take dramatic shots of divers breaking the surface or gliding through the water. A good swimmer can do an underwater ballet or a handstand on the bottom of the pool for you.

You may want to reread the information on underwater equipment and its use in the *Equipment* and *Underwater Photography* chapters.

Seeing and Breathing—For a clear underwater view, wear a diving mask. It offers the additional advantage of keeping irritating chlorine and other pools chemicals out of your eyes.

We find a snorkel useful in underwater photography in a pool. It is a breathing tube that extends from your mouth to above the water surface. It permits you to stay just below the surface for extended periods. This is helpful because your diving mask is likely to fog over each time your face surfaces.

Mobility—Fins on your feet increase your mobility dramatically. They enable you to move rapidly and with great precision from place to place.

Daylight—If you want to shoot natural-light portraits under water, do it at the shallow end of the pool. The less water the daylight has to penetrate, the more light you'll get on the subject and the less color imbalance—toward blue—will show in your photos.

To get the best lighting on a face, have the subject tilt the head slightly upward toward the surface. To make posing and composing the image easier for you, it's advisable to have your subject hold onto something, such as a pool ladder.

Artificial Light—Pool lights are generally built into the side of a pool. Depending on how you position your subject, you can take portraits lit frontally or from the side. Or, you can make dramatic silhouettes against the light. To get the full benefit of the illumination, have the subject near the light source.

Underwater pool lighting generally uses tungsten bulbs. To get the most accurate color rendition, use a tungsten-balanced color-slide film. If you want to use daylight film, use an appropriate color conversion filter in the 80 series. If you don't, your pictures may appear excessively reddish.

This photo is a fine expression of "fun at the pool." The dripping hair, the splashing water and the glistening bodies all help to put life into the picture. Photo from Southern Stock Photos.

Action—Underwater action can make for interesting photographs. You can record on film dramatic turns by a swimmer at the end of the pool. Or, you can shoot a diver as he penetrates the surface.

Safety is an important consideration in any water activity. If you shoot underwater action, be sure you are out of harm's way, both for yourself and your "performer." Remember that, because of light refraction, your position under water is deceptive to a viewer from above.

Bubble Trails—When a swimmer or diver glides through a pool, he leaves a trail of churned-up water. The trail adds a sensation of action to pictures, so try to include it.

WATER SLIDE

A pool with a water slide offers additional possibilities for photography. Children come down forward or backward, often with arms and legs outstretched. Expressions can register any emotion from terror to delight. Capture the action—both while the subject is on the slide and when he splashes into the water.

To capture all the action, use a motor drive. For close detail use a telephoto lens.